Design Technology in Contemporary Architectural Practice

Design Technology in Contemporary Architectural Practice lifts the curtain to unveil how eleven world-leading design studios integrate technology (such as computational design, BIM, and digital fabrication) as part of their day-to-day design exploration and delivery. Via first-hand accounts, the book offers rare insights about how these firms apply technology to purposefully disrupt and support their creative design processes in order to then explore how technology can be integrated on an organisational level. The resulting practice stories are loosely tied to four chapters that discuss how Design Technology corresponds to studio culture, collaboration and delivery protocols, business opportunities, knowledge sharing, staff empowerment, and more.

The author is less interested in presenting the latest and greatest tools than in focusing on cultural and organisational challenges and opportunities. This book benefits both the professional market (such as design firms reflecting on their technology use), as well as the academic context (with its critical reflection on the interface between design process and technology support). Stories from the following design firms are included:

Coop Himmelb(l)au
Foster + Partners
Bjarke Ingels Group (BIG)
Zaha Hadid Architects
Diller Scofidio + Renfo
Heatherwick Studio
Morphosis Architects
SO-IL
Woods Bagot
Herzog & de Meuron
LASSA

Dominik Holzer is Associate Professor in Digital Architectural Design at the University of Melbourne (Australia) where he teaches architecture, construction, and architectural engineering. An architect by training, Dominik researches, educates, and consults across domains within the built environment. His work centres around the cultural and organisational opportunities and challenges associated with technology-use in contemporary practice.

In parallel to his efforts in academia, Dominik established AEC Connect as an independent strategic BIM, Digital Engineering, and Design Technology consultancy, operating since 2009 in the Asia-Pacific region.

He frequently presents and publishes on Design Technology, (post) Digital Practice, and transdisciplinary collaboration. His *BIM Manager's Handbook* (2016) has received wide praise from both industry and academia. The topics covered in his publications draw on the expertise he has established over the past two decades, and his approachable writing style makes them accessible for a wide audience.

Design Technology in Contemporary Architectural Practice

Dominik Holzer

Foreword by Mark Burry

LONDON AND NEW YORK

Designed cover image: Photography © Dominik Holzer.

First published 2023
by Routledge
4 Park Square, Milton Park, Abingdon, Oxon OX14 4RN

and by Routledge
605 Third Avenue, New York, NY 10158

Routledge is an imprint of the Taylor & Francis Group, an informa business

© 2023 Dominik Holzer

The right of Dominik Holzer to be identified as author of this work has been asserted in accordance with sections 77 and 78 of the Copyright, Designs and Patents Act 1988.

All rights reserved. No part of this book may be reprinted or reproduced or utilised in any form or by any electronic, mechanical, or other means, now known or hereafter invented, including photocopying and recording, or in any information storage or retrieval system, without permission in writing from the publishers.

Trademark notice: Product or corporate names may be trademarks or registered trademarks, and are used only for identification and explanation without intent to infringe.

British Library Cataloguing-in-Publication Data
A catalogue record for this book is available from the British Library

Library of Congress Cataloging-in-Publication Data
Names: Holzer, Dominik, author.
Title: Design technology in contemporary architectural practice /
 Dominik Holzer.
Description: Abingdon, Oxon : Routledge, 2023. | Includes bibliographical
 references and index.
Identifiers: LCCN 2022056078 (print) | LCCN 2022056079 (ebook) |
 ISBN 9781138624535 (hardback) | ISBN 9781138624542 (paperback) |
 ISBN 9780429460722 (ebook)
Subjects: LCSH: Architectural design—Data processing.
Classification: LCC NA2728 .H65 2023 (print) | LCC NA2728 (ebook) |
 DDC 720.285—dc23/eng/20221125
LC record available at https://lccn.loc.gov/2022056078
LC ebook record available at https://lccn.loc.gov/2022056079

ISBN: 978-1-138-62453-5 (hbk)
ISBN: 978-1-138-62454-2 (pbk)
ISBN: 978-0-429-46072-2 (ebk)

DOI: 10.4324/9780429460722

Typeset in Avenir
by Apex CoVantage, LLC

This book is dedicated to my son Ryu, whom I am very proud of

Contents

Foreword (by Mark Burry)	ix
Preface	xiii
Acknowledgements	xvii
List of Acronyms and Abbreviations	xix

1. Introduction – Defining Design Technology — 1

1.1 Background to Design Technology	2
1.2 How the 'Information Age' Has Transformed Architectural Design Practice	3
Practice Insert: **Coop Himmelb(l)au**	5
1.3 Computational Design in Architecture Practice – A Brief History	14
Practice Insert: **Foster + Partners**	**19**
1.4 The Proliferation of Parametric Design and Scripting	28
1.5 Object-oriented Design Documentation Going Mainstream	29
1.6 Digital Models for Structural and Environmental Performance Feedback	30
Practice Insert: **BIG – Bjarke Ingels Group**	34

2. Positioning Technology Within Design Practice — 41

2.1 The Ambivalent Relationship Between Architects and (Design) Technology	41
2.2 Becoming Strategic About Technology Choices	44
Practice Insert: **Zaha Hadid Architects**	46
2.3 Matching Studio Culture With Technology Support	55
Practice Insert: **Diller Scofidio + Renfo**	58
2.4 Addressing Design Technology on an Organisational Level	66
2.5 Setting Up and Positioning Design Technology Within the Office Structure	66
Practice Insert: **Heatherwick Studio**	71
2.6 Project Support	78
Practice Insert: **Morphosis Architects**	82
2.7 Design Technology: Liaising With Practice Leadership	90
2.8 The Next Level – Design Technology as a Business Opportunity	92
Practice Insert: **SO-IL**	94

3. Tooling 101

3.1 Seeking Alignment Between Design Process
and Tools 101
3.2 Tool: From Drafting Support to Decision Support
(and More?) 103
Practice Insert: **Woods Bagot** 106
3.3 More Flexible/Smaller/Lighter 115
3.4 The Virtual Office 117
Practice Insert: **Herzog & de Meuron** **120**
3.5 File to Fabrication 128
Practice Insert: **LASSA** 133
3.6 Convergence – Tooling Across Domains 141
3.7 Design Technology, Semiotics, and Human Behaviour! 142

4. Moving Forward 145

Interview With Four Leading Design Technologists 145

Index 155

Foreword (by Mark Burry)

Having played some small part in Dominik's later academic and professional formation, I am delighted to be penning the opening to this remarkable book, a labour of love from a widely experienced and talented individual.

In 2002, two decades prior to writing this foreword, I gave a 'Friday afternoon presentation' to Alsop Architects' staff. The topic was our adoption of parametric design at the Sagrada Família Basilica technical office and how we melded Gaudí's singular design process with emerging digital technologies of the day. I outlined the advantages of their take-up and development for which we had unexpectedly become renowned during the previous fifteen years. Gaudí's challenge to his successors begged solutions from us that extended our human capability, and Avant Garde practices of the day were interested in learning more.

I was there at the instigation of the author of this book, Dr Dominik Holzer, who was then an associate at Alsop Architects at a relatively young age. In terms of the migration of digital technologies towards being more than just drafting tools, these were early days still, but there were already considerable schisms emerging where debate about technique risked sidelining the weightier matters of style and composition that had previously dominated our discourse.

At my presentation, we discussed the relationship between the rapidly developing Design Technology arena and traditional architectural practice – at that time parametric design, 3D printing, photorealistic rendering, scripting, Machine Learning, and 4D real-time simulation were very much in their infancy but rapidly coming into wider view. To some, Design Technology pointed towards a future where the handcraft of practice and all its inefficiencies would go the way of log tables and the slide rule for the engineer – formally vital tools for performing calculations in the predigital era but completely redundant for that purpose today. My apologies to any young reader forced to look up these relatively recent obsolete mathematical and algebraic tools before, first, the digital calculator, and then the personal computer arrived on the scene during the 1970s.

For others, Design Technology still points to a far less exciting and wholly more worrying prospect in which the eye-mind-hand connection fades away and with it the time-honoured reflexivity that the carefully handcrafted drawing and modelling afford. This more traditionally grounded community has been very influential in many schools of architecture which continue today promoting learning about how our discipline used to practice architecture rather than how we practice today, let alone how we might be working in the near future.

In terms of design, technology, and architecture, there is at least one other community who keep their feet in both camps. To them,

Design Technology heralds an era of architectural design practice enriched by digital assistance, augmenting rather than supplanting artistic traditions, an era where practitioners will increasingly get more out of their working day, whether as conceptual designers, design developers, design managers, or building overseers. This is a good point to give a shout-out to the roles of universities in Design Technology, and the emergence of transdisciplinary practice, both of which this book alludes to implicitly and explicitly. There are competing definitions of the term *transdisciplinary practice*, but it is commonly taken to mean at least two university-based disciplines and one party external to academia tackling a problem together and seeking options worthy of further enquiry rather than a single solution. Given that the role of the enlightened professional architect (as opposed to the dedicated academic) has traditionally tackled design challenges following this model, as problems become more wicked, Design Technology becomes more necessary.

While it might be logical to direct a book on Design Technology towards those who take a more neutral but enlightened position, this book targets all three communities – conservative, enlightened, and zealot – in ways that allow everyone to access a subject that has been rather hidden from view both in curricular and in the way practices typically organise themselves. It focuses on the reader who is curious about Design Technology per se, how it has influenced a sample of outstanding architectural practices for our time – large and small, with both implied and actual pathways for its adoption. Not least in this community of inquiring adopters was the late Will Alsop, leader of the practice at which I was presenting my thoughts for the future to the author of this book and his colleagues. I was staggered to discover that Will Alsop had co-opted Adobe Illustrator™, of all software, for design exploration, translating his inimitable flair from the easel to the digital canvas.

Whether Will Alsop would have accepted the label of 'design technologist' is moot, but such labels beg the question: who is the design technologist in any practice, and what exactly is their role? What the book reveals is that Design Technology can be part of what you do and how you practice. Equally, there are individuals who describe themselves as 'design technologists', and there are practices that that install departments with the specific role to provide Design Technology services albeit not necessarily titled as such. This book cuts to the quick in seeking to define both the subdiscipline as well as the person. Revealing insights come from people such as Martha Tsigkari at Foster + Partners, Shane Burger at Woods Bagot, Keranza Harris at Morphosis, Shajay Bhooshan at Zaha Hadid Architects, and Matthew Ostrow (formerly) at Diller Scofidio + Renfo – leading examples of design technologists who have taken on this role in practice but from widely varying backgrounds with quite different interactions with the practice leaders. There is a small elephant in the room in this regard when we consider the origins of computer-aided drafting (CAD) and its reluctant insinuation into school curricula. There were few heroes to proselytise the design benefits of the take-up of digitalisation; rather, they were less design-credentialled colleagues whose focus was on office efficiency and productivity. I believe that this has taken place at quite a cost with insufficient graduates emerging with the requisite scripting and parametric design skills and, as a consequence, too few practices aware of the design lift that skilful application of digital technologies give beyond BIM and design documentation. This book greatly helps rehabilitate the role of technology within the design arena by drawing on adept practicing design technologists and leaders of Design Technology in practices that have been making a difference along the way with great architecture and hard-won digital know-how and flair.

The author brings a strong designerly perspective to this survey of digital practice coupled with deep knowledge of the evolving design technologies that have been masterly applied across the globe. At TU Vienna, Dominik pulled against the 'classical' education devoted to the analogue architectural representation of ideas and aspirations and their conversion into buildings that students were expected to undergo. He had already identified the possibilities of digitalised design practice and had participated in counter-current intensive studios led by luminaries such as Carl Chu and Cecil Balmond in the late 1990s, ultimately leading to his final year thesis on 'Open Geometry, Informal Topology', while embedded with Lars Spuybroek at NOX in Rotterdam.

Dominik has made an amalgam of academic teaching and research with his professional practice as a leading Design Technology expert, focusing on the promotion of high-end technology across design, engineering, construction, and the operation of buildings throughout their life beyond completion. Not only has he enjoyed four years at Alsop Architects, then a globally leading design practice, he has also spent three years with the internationally renowned engineering firm of Arup as an 'embedded practitioner' while undertaking his master's and his PhD at the Spatial Information Architecture Laboratory (SIAL) at Melbourne's RMIT University 2004–2010. A hotbed of applied Design Technology, SIAL's mission was to share architectural and engineering practice transdisciplinary digital design research with masters and PhD candidates from all design disciplines, engineering, and computer science. He regards his time at SIAL as a uniquely formative experience, and it was there as part of his doctoral studies that he explored ways to streamline the workflow of multidisciplinary design teams using high-end Design Technology. This gave him the opportunity to focus on knowledge exchange and project management for complex large-scale building projects requiring sophisticated cross-professional collaborations using evolving tools that were transforming business. Before initiating his highly successful consultancy offering expert advice on best-practice data exchange and the alignment of inter- and intra-organisational processes associated to project delivery and operation in the built environment, he enjoyed four years as Design Technology Director at BVN Architecture, a large multicity Australian practice where he developed their national strategy for introducing 3D, BIM, and technological innovation to their practice. In this role, he led their adoption of new processes and software while overseeing the BIM execution on all their projects. This unusually broad experience across the design and engineering professions complements his academic career currently as Associate Professor in Digital Architecture at the University of Melbourne.

In short, with both a *design* and *technology* background, a career trifecta of practice, consulting, and academia, the author is in a unique position to garner real world stories from close to a dozen makers and shakers who have helped shape the contemporary built environment during the transition from traditional to digital design practice. As a result, this book of itself is unique for the range of perspectives it provides in the Design Technology field. Rather than pontificate from an academic pulpit, far-reaching perspectives have been drawn out from industry leaders and beautifully distilled, bookended between a contextual setting and background and an adroit conversation among four leading Design Technology thinkers who muse on where Design Technology is going and what it will lead to. Prominent within the background context and speculative finale sits the main course: a series of skilfully led conversations between the author and practice-based Design Technology leaders who demonstrate not only how wide the field of Design Technology has become from a relatively modest scope and ambitions three decades ago but also how deep they run too, as we start to see the influence of Artificial Intelligence (AI) and other technologies become more evident. The book shares the views from both large and small practices, heavy hitters who began their successful careers in analogue times (Coop Himmelb(l)au, Zaha Hadid Architects, Herzog & de Meuron) and others that are relatively young, small, and agile (SO-IL and LASSA). Some of the practices adopt Design Technology as an adjunct for their *modus operandi* rather than as a driver (BIG, DS+R, and Heatherwick Studio), while for others Design Technology takes centre stage (Morphosis, Woods Bagot, Foster + Partners).

Through the interviews of both pioneers and young digirati, his book provides a great here-and-now account of the state of the art with a subtle reference to history. So, while being of its time and very much cutting-edge, its authority and deep international dive unpacking the status quo insures the book's longevity despite the fast-changing digital landscape. The insights revealed and discussed here will be just as compelling to a reader in fifty years' time as they are today; its expert encapsulation of the state of play is in a professional arena that could self-destruct unless it takes heed of this *Meisterwerk*'s key messages. Subscribing to the cyclical view of history and cognisant of the architectural profession's tendency to reinvent wheels, for a future reader revisiting this account of the evolution of digital in architectural practice today that remains fairly resistant to change, here are the ingredients of an antidote to conservatism – valuable pointers showing how enlightened practitioners absorb change in the manner of Will Alsop and the latter-day titans unpacked within these pages.

Preface

The idea behind this book evolved over a period of over ten to fifteen years, partly influenced by my role as Design Technology Director of a large architecture firm, as well as my research about the transformative character of digital processes on design practice. I have always been fascinated by the cultural impact of technology on the way architects and their collaborators advance projects. The key questions I have been asking are: how do the world's most prolific architects apply technology as part of their design and delivery processes, and what in-house support infrastructure do they set up to accomplish this endeavour?

Over large portions of the past century, the use of technology in architectural design has predominantly focused on increasing efficiency in drafting, visualisation, and the facilitation of more streamlined communication across project stakeholders. This is still a major factor in what technology offers us today. Yet the past thirty years have also seen a major expansion from the main emphasis on documentation, visualisation, data storage, and communication (often facilitated via Information Technology (IT) specialists). More recently, Design Technology increasingly facilitates deeper cross-fertilisation between technology and exploratory design processes, all the way towards fabrication and post-delivery/maintenance. In the future, technology promises to become an even stronger design partner via data analytics and the use of artificial intelligence (AI). As 'on-the-floor IT' support is increasingly getting backgrounded (with many design teams relying on remote-access and cloud-based support), Design Technology (DT) specialists make their mark on practice as they help transform the industry.

At no point has the relevance of Design Technology become more apparent than in the role it played in offering a lifeline to design firms in times of COVID, where remote working had become the de facto standard for many architecture studios around the world. Without the input by Design Technology specialists to help 'virtualise practice', it would likely have been impossible for many firms to survive. Some of the emergency measures implemented during COVID now appear to be here to stay, thereby speeding up technology adoption in unexpected ways. Examples include the increased reliance on online design meetings or the acceptance of virtual and augmented reality (VR/AR) as a mainstream addition to 3D model reviews.

In this book, I juxtapose a broader exploration of Design Technology with 'practice stories' from eleven renowned design firms. These stories are slotted at strategic points between four main chapters in order to allow the reader to associate the principles behind Design Technology with their hands-on application.

Chapter 1 sets the scene for Design Technology and the way it is incorporated into current design firms. The chapter investigates the emergence of Design Technology within architecture practice from a historical perspective but also by highlighting different streams of the design inquiry and resolution it supports beyond its original application in design visualisation and documentation. From parametric design and scripting to BIM and Digital Engineering, all the way to Design Technology in support of building performance optimisation. In Chapter 2, I delve deeper in the organisational context of design firms as I scrutinise the affordances on practice to manage their Design Technology implementation strategically. Here, I focus on Design Technology in the context of studio culture (and matching technology choices), proliferation within an organisation, the setup of a support infrastructure, and on-project implementation. The chapter also focuses on crucial interfaces between Design Technology and practice leadership, as well as the business opportunities it may present to those adopting Design Technology.

The focus of Chapter 3 lies on tools and digital applications that have most prominently emerged in Design Technology over the past few decades. I first discuss the alignment of architectural design processes with a matching tool selection and then explore the development of tools from drafting to decision support. I explain how users' preferences for tools have changed over time, resulting in more flexible and targeted applications and tool ecologies. Chapter 3 further outlines the convergence between different types of applications as currently experienced in practice, and it touches on trends such as tools used to explore (and design with) human behaviour. After introducing Design Technology tools in use for setting up and operating a 'virtual office', the chapter ends by scrutinising current applications that assist in transitioning from exploratory design to documentation and finally those that allow for a direct interface with fabrication processes.

The book concludes with a short, yet pointed Chapter 4, titled: 'Moving Forward'. There, I invite four leading experts to share their insights on Design Technology's current best practice. All four of them approach this from different angles, and they join me in speculating about how design practices will likely approach Design Technology in the near future. The chapter offers a fascinating outlook at cutting-edge approaches with provocative and pointed comments about things to come.

Despite the fact that I have been deeply involved in the way Design Technology has unfolded in practice for two to three decades, writing this book has offered me surprising new insights and has taken me on a journey of discovery that I am excited to share with you. My understanding of contemporary issues related to Design Technology has influenced the questions I asked the leading design firms represented here. Their responses have helped me to firm up the strategies and approaches I describe in this book. The eleven practices opened their doors to grant me a glimpse behind the curtain of their otherwise secluded operations. The result is a fascinating account on where Design Technology is positioned within these firms and how it assists them to achieve their creative output.

Not one Design Technology strategy is like another. With this book, I therefore celebrate the diversity of approaches reflected by leading global architects and the Design Technology experts they work with. There is new knowledge to be gained and many lessons to be learned from these design innovators and creative thinkers.

Dominik Holzer

▲ Figure 0.1

3D printed working models, project progression.
Morphosis Architects

Acknowledgements

The author acknowledges the contribution from Mark Burry for the pointed contextualisation of the book in his foreword.

In addition, the author wants to thank all those who have contributed to this book via their feedback during interviews in various practices, these include but are not limited to the following individuals:

Coop Himmelb(l)au: Karolin Schmidbaur and Markus Prossnigg
Foster + Partners: Martha Tsigkari and Rafe Bertram
Bjarke Ingels Group (BIG): Oliver Thomas
Zaha Hadid Architects (ZHA): Patrik Schumacher, Charles Walker, and
    Shajay Bhooshan
Diller Scofidio + Renfo (DS+R): Ricardo Scofidio and Matthew Ostrow
Heatherwick Studio: Pablo Zamorano
Morphosis Architects: Thom Mayne and Kerenza Harris
SO-IL: Jing Liu and Ted Baab
Woods Bagot: Shane Burger
Herzog & de Meuron (H&deM): Steffen Riegas and Michael Drobnik
LASSA: Theo Sarantoglou Lalis

In addition, I would like to acknowledge the contribution of those individuals who shared their insights and supported me in writing this book: Fabian Scheurer (Design-to-Production), Daniel Davis (Hassell), Jon Mirtchin (Geometry Gym), Nate Miller (the Proving Ground), Paul Poinet, Don Bates, Paul Loh.

Acronyms and Abbreviations

AA	Architectural Association (London)
AI	Artificial Intelligence
AR	Augmented Reality
BIM	Building Information Modelling or Building Information Model
CAAD	Computer Aided Architectural Design
CAD	Computer Aided Design
CFD	Computational Fluid Dynamics
CNC	Computer Numerical Construction
DS+R	Diller Scofidio + Renfo
DT	Design Technology
GH	Grasshopper™ (parametric design software by McNeel)
H&deM	Herzog & de Meuron
IAAC	Institute for Advanced Architecture of Catalonia
IT	Information Technology
R&D	Research and Development
SIAL	Spatial Information Architecture Lab
TU	Technische Universität
VR	Virtual Reality
ZHA	Zaha Hadid Architects

Chapter 1

Introduction – Defining Design Technology

In 1984, legendary jazz pianist Herbie Hancock invited his friend and equally renowned composer Quincy Jones over to his studio for a jam session, as captured in the documentary *I Love Quincy*.[1] At first, the documentary seems to capture nothing more than a moment between two artists, who had known each other for decades. Yet, this time, something was different: Hancock introduces Jones to his 'new toy' – a Fairlight CMI (Computer Music Instrument). The 28-megabyte synthesizer comes with a touchscreen monitor and a digital stylus that allowed Hancock to program in sounds that interacted with his keyboard (a highly revolutionary process back in the early 1980s). At one point, Hancock demonstrates for Jones the sampling and sequencing functions of CMI's software interface to create new rhythms and soundscapes. Jones is instantly drawn to Hancock's blending of analogue keyboard improvisations with digital sounds, achieving real-time feedback between the two. He refers to it as 'sculpting a pure electric signal into something of beauty'. Jones soon masters the controls of the CMI software, and the two musicians can be seen jamming together, moving fluidly across analogue and digital media.

What fascinates about this 'timepiece' of electronic music is the ease with which two of the most prolific musicians of their time (both deeply rooted in 'analogue ways of production') manage to interact with computer programs to improvise and explore new ideas and compose fascinating sounds on the fly.

▲ Figure 1.1

Extracts from the documentary *I Love Quincy*.
© Eric Lipmann

Around that time, architects also started to experiment with computational tools to support their design and delivery processes. Yet, thirty to forty years on,

---

1 Available at: www.openculture.com/2012/10/watch_herbie_hancock_rock_out_on_an_early_synthesizer_on_sesame_street_1983.html

one would be hard pressed to find a similar level of intuitive interaction between architectural designers and their computers. By nature, there exist good reasons why computer-aided musical improvisation can result in spontaneous master-pieces, yet such ad hoc output is nearly impossible to achieve for architects: there is simply too much pre- and post-rationalisation across multiple stakeholders involved in architectural design to allow for such immediate output. That said, Design Technology has been transforming many aspects of contemporary archi-tectural practice, and it has had a dramatic impact on the architecture profes-sion more generally. With blended analogue–digital 'jam sessions' still seeming out of reach, architects have nevertheless learned to integrate digital Design Technology into their everyday work processes to support both their creative and their design documentation sides.

1.1   Background to Design Technology

It comes as no surprise that technology has had a major impact on archi-tecture practice over the past forty to fifty years. Gone are the days when architects spent countless hours on T-squares, scratching excess Rotring ink off their drawings, and using their projection and colouring skills to develop a fabulous perspective drawing of their project. Computer Aided Architectural Design, Digital Architecture, or Computational Design (name it whatever you want) has transformed not only how we design but what we design. For many architecture firms in the developed world, running their practice without digital tools and associated infrastructure would appear not only unthinkable but also unsustainable.

Countless publications have addressed the use of computational means to assist architects in their design and delivery of projects. This publication does not aim to replicate or consolidate their findings. Instead, Design Technology in Contemporary Practice offers a unique insight into the transformative aspect of technology on the way practices are organised and run. Initially seen as a sub-component of Information Technology (IT), Design Technology has by now estab-lished itself as stand-alone stream within practice. But what exactly is Design Technology, and what is its relationship to Digital Architecture or even to CAAD?

Under the banner of Design Technology, practices consolidate the activi-ties and processes they engage in, plus the tools and techniques they apply to design and deliver their projects with the use of digital technology! In this post-digital era, the resulting architecture does not become 'digital' just because digital tools have assisted to realise it. We are absorbing digital processes in our designerly workflow and position them among non-digital processes as a matter of course. What ultimately counts is that architects, as designers, use the most appropriate means to explore and express their designs at any point on a project.

Technology is changing. Over the past decade, design-related activi-ties increasingly get supported using digital technology. Practices now aim to channel their efforts to consolidate their technology use and to converge differ-ent streams of inquiry into a more holistic approach. Still, several distinct technol-ogy-centric roles and specialisations have emerged such as the 'computational designer' (using parametric techniques, rule-based design, scripting, simulation, and analysis), the BIM Expert (responsible for object-oriented modelling and coordination), the Visualisation expert (spanning from simple 3D imagery to ani-mations and Virtual/Augmented Reality), or the Fabrication Expert (using rapid prototyping, additive manufacturing, and/or robotics). What connects them all is the way they connect and use data to expand on their firm's design and delivery capability.

2   CHAPTER 1 Introduction – Defining Design Technology

One other key aspect to consider, when addressing Design Technology within an organisational context, is the inherent lifespan of any approach taken. Managing Design Technology is about striking a balance between the possible and the feasible. Compared to other aspects of architecture practice, changes to technology occur very rapidly. For those looking after Design Technology, it is not so much about keeping up with all these changes but about finding alignment between practice culture and technological advance, whilst considering budget implications. It helps to be aware of the broader context of technology uptake and its proliferation across architecture practice in the past decades.

1.2 How the 'Information Age' Has Transformed Architectural Design Practice

Looking around in any architecture firm, one sees how things have been changing. The days of hand-drafting are long gone, and computer screens now form the major interface of designers to advance their work computationally. Two-dimensional sketching and physical model making still complement the otherwise digital workflow that architecture practices have signed up to. Today, technology plays a major role in design practice, but its focus has shifted: in the past, architects used technology predominantly to increase efficiency in their work and to speed up their design documentation and visualisation via Information Technology. Now the emphasis lies on allowing architects to expand their design options, evaluate different scenarios on the fly, and push for novel solutions that would otherwise be very difficult (if not impossible) to achieve without the help of Design Technology.

At best, advances in computing power and networking speed facilitate technological solutions that are intuitive, easy to learn, exhaustive, and aligned with designerly thinking. Design options can be generated on the fly, evaluated in real time, and reconfigured quickly to respond to new inputs (from a team) whatever they may be. We are increasingly closing the gap between tools that allow for such open-ended, exploratory processes, and the design output-focused applications that ultimately drive the creation of documentation sets of direct links to fabrication/assembly equipment.

Back to practice itself: how are advances in technology changing how design firms operate? What does the increased shift from technology as background support to technology as enabler signify for the future of architectural practice? And how are studios responding to these developments on the design, organisational, and management levels? For design firms, the integration of Information Technology (IT) into their office structure has always remained a sideshow that had to be considered as part of budgeting and staffing. As long as the relevant software was installed and available, the hardware worked trouble-free, and the network was functioning well, nobody cared how it was achieved. For most design practices, their IT setup never really affected the way they designed or the way they delivered their documentation (beyond IT's enabling function). This could not be more different from the way Design Technology (DT) is integrated in today's practice. Whilst still depending on a good interface with IT, DT ties directly into the core activities carried out by architects, and it has a major impact on the quality and efficiency of how architects carry out their daily design tasks. Even further, DT has the potential to introduce major innovations and change to design practices.

Design Technology allows architects to simplify the complexity/complicatedness inherent to certain types of projects. It allows them to make sense out of calculus-intensive coordination of information and to otherwise automate

CHAPTER 1 Introduction – Defining Design Technology   **3** processes that are considered tedious and time-consuming. That way, Design Technology increases efficiencies, enables experimentation, facilitates the quest for innovation, and ultimately allows designers to step away from the beaten track that relies heavily on precedence.

In reflection: for many architects, Computer Aided Architectural Design (CAAD) was mainly a means to an end in order to document more efficiently. Today, 2D documents are still the key medium to communicate with clients, consultants, and contractors, as architects, engineers, and contractors still print out drawings to mark them up and to share information with others. Yet in the background, a silent revolution has taken place that has turned the way some architects operate upside down. Among the earliest adopters of a highly bespoke use of Design Technology are Coop Himmelb(l)au, who have continuously transformed their practice since the late 1960s until today.

Physical model

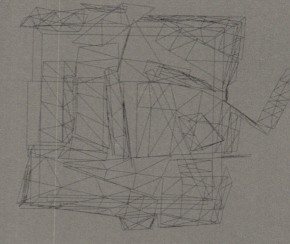

Computer model

▲ Figure 1.2
Groninger Museum, Groningen, The Netherlands (1993–1994), physical and digital model.
© Coop Himmelb(l)au

COOP HIMMELB(L)AU

▲ Figure 1.3
Groninger Museum, Groningen, The Netherlands (1993–1994), digital model scan.
© Coop Himmelb(l)au

PRACTICE INSERT: Coop Himmelb(l)au

Coop Himmelb(l)au have been a fixture on the global architecture scene with an oeuvre that spans well over five decades. Within that period, they have always questioned conventions, and they keep pushing the agenda of what is possible. As a matter of fact, Design Technology has always played an important role, assisting them in realising their bold ideas. The practice was one of the earliest adopters of 3D technology (in terms of both modelling and scanning), and they work closely with contractors and fabricators to streamline the process from conception to realisation.

Coop's Design Partner Karolin Schmidbaur and Managing Partner Markus Prossnigg explain this in greater detail:

What role does Design Technology play at Coop Himmelb(l)au? How do you implement it to support your distinctive design approach?

KS: Coop Himmelb(l)au started using digital 3D models for documentation and fabrication over twenty-five years ago. That said, our projects are idea driven, and we always had a vested interest in innovative Design Technology to understand how we can realise those ideas. We built our first 'digital project' in 1993–1994. In our Los Angeles office at that time, we scanned the physical model of the Groningen Museum with a space arm, developed it via a 3D model, and built straight off that model.

Despite being highly advanced in using digital tools, we never stopped making physical models. We continue to build physical models even though we now also apply an array of high-end technology from parametric modelling to robotic fabrication and AI. In the end it is about using the most suitable tool for any given task, wherever appropriate. This is why I refer to our tool use as 'ideas motivated'!

Naturally, if new technology becomes available or shows particular promise, we will experiment with it to explore what it might offer us.

How is Design Technology integrated at Coop Himmelb(l)au on an organisational level?

MP: We have project architects and design architects who spearhead our projects.

KS: Their split in responsibilities could be compared to the split between the left and right side of the brain: one covers function and form (how the internal organisation of the building gets translated into its morphology), and the other looks more after the function and technical aspects of the project. The design architect coordinates the design teams, the model makers, and the 3D designers.

▲ Figure 1.4

Deep Himmelblau, model to image.
© Coop Himmelb(l)au

The project architect rather looks after the organisation of the building, as well as its building systems, and the coordination of consultants.

Design architect/project architect staffing is mainly derived from our general knowledge pool, whereas the specialists typically do not get associated to a specific project team (unless it is very large project where we would need a dedicated BIM resource for three years). The Design Technology specialists cut across teams; they are either available in the office or contracted in on a need basis.

MP: The setup varies from project to project. As an example, we invested intensely into the use of Digital Project™ a few years ago in order to evaluate how the tool can augment our capabilities. On other projects, however, we focused on the use of 'constructive-Rhino™', which was quite elaborate.

Which management structures do you have in place to effectively apply Design Technology at Coop Himmelb(l)au? Please mention human resources as well as hardware/infrastructure available.

MP: We do not employ a dedicated DT team; our specialists cover this sort of work like performance optimisation in addition to other computational work using Rhino/Grasshopper™/scripting/fabrication.

KS: There are certain skills that form part of the basic expectations we have from anyone who works with us, whether they come straight from university or worked elsewhere before. Part of those skills refer to the ability to model and sketch in 3D, scripting, digital fabrication, etc. Most people in our office have those skills. Next, we employ experts whose skills exceed that level. They work on bespoke issues via programming, robotic interfaces, AI, etc. Some might lean more towards specialisation on design and planning aspects, others on construction/delivery aspects.

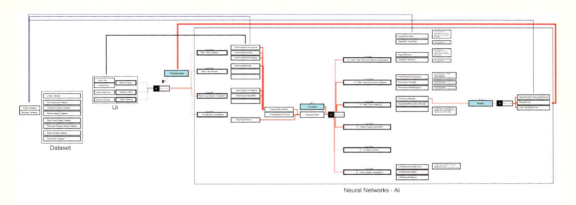

▲ Figure 1.5

Deep Himmelblau, Roadmap.
© Coop Himmelb(l)au

Are there sometimes any cultural clashes between the design approach and Technology/Technologists at Coop Himmelb(l)au?

KS: In principle, our process is an open process – open to any new idea. The idea then gets tested against our guiding principles on the project. We repeatedly set up research groups who are dedicated to explore design issues in a self-motivated manner. Their work is conducted to inform and advance projects and ideas relevant to contemporary issues on a meta level.

We do not include technology in our design process for technology's sake. It is typically a means to an end; a way to enable or facilitate what we want to achieve.

How do you manage to achieve the high level of quality in construction execution as seen in some of your recent projects?

MP: We push the client from the early design phases to work with prototypes for – let's say – 'façade cladding' elements. Alternatively, we build an entire component of the building as a sample.

KS: Our 3D Design Masterfiles are not just rough 3D representations, but they are highly detailed virtual construction models that contain precise information about primary/secondary structural components, as well as cladding systems.

MP: We consider innovative technology as an enabler to allow the architect to regain more control over the delivery of projects. In Shenzhen at the MOCAPE we used Digital Project to test what we can influence with this tool. We consciously used Digital Project over several phases of the project to enable us to influence the construction aspect of the project in a way we could not easily have accomplished otherwise. A key aspect of achieving the level of precision inherent to the construction of the Shenzhen project was the fact that they fabricated off our models one to one.

KS: Via the 3D virtual model, we are able to resolve not only fabrication-related issues but also complex geometrical problems.

M: In the back of our mind, we know that the computational tools we apply force us to work more precisely and think through issues more thoroughly. One starts to work through issues in an algorithmic sense, as well as considering performance optimisation; overall working in 3D pushes you to set up rules and adhere to those as part of the design process.

As part of this process, how much do you bring in the expertise of your key (e.g., structural engineering) collaborators?

MP: As an example: we have grown very familiar with the engineering firm Bollinger Grohman in the past, and we know them well enough by now to develop concepts jointly. They not only play an important role due to their understanding of our distinct approach to architecture (with lots of exposed structural systems) but also to develop intelligent and efficient building systems that are technically interesting and can be realised within our budget constraints.

▼ Figure 1.6

BWM Welt, Munich, Germany (2001–2007), physical model filming, Coop Himmelb(l)au.
© Markus Pillhofer

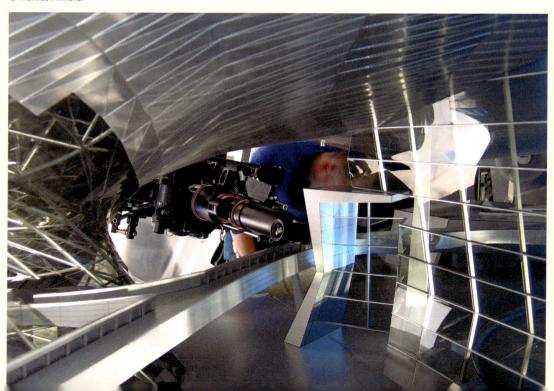

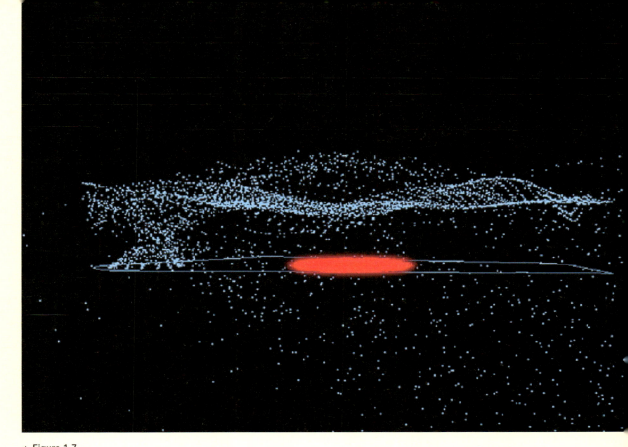

▲ Figure 1.7
BWM Welt, Munich, Germany (2001–2007), dynamic particle simulation.
© Coop Himmelb(l)au

Tell me about the interplay between Design and Technology from your perspective. Can you take inspiration from the innovation potential facilitated by some of the design and fabrication tools you use?

KS: We clearly do. We often carry out self-initiated research projects in the office that are used to try new things out. The results from these studies find their way back into actual projects as a matter of course.

MP: This also relates to the kind of analyses we conduct. Like for instance the effect of wind or solar studies on a project's morphology. Our in-house specialists explore those options in a way that allows us to derive additional benefits from the technology we apply.

Could the feedback you get from this type of computational analysis reach as far as to make you reconsider some primary design decisions made earlier (without compromising the project's program)?

MP: Absolutely, we are happy to weave in guidance from what we find out in the analysis, and Wolf and the rest of the team are open to accommodate changes that are suggested by this sort of performance feedback.

KS: . . . but you do not just change your design in the virtual model and then simply trust the output. You always have to go back into the physical realm to verify the results. If they are not pleasing aesthetically and functionally, we rerun the iterative physical-virtual modelling process until we get where we want to be. We can now optimise a façade's subdivision tiles using scripting methods and to then compare ten variations.

PRACTICE INSERT: Coop Himmelb(l)au

▲ Figure 1.8

Performance overlay on physical working models at the Coop Himmelb(l)au office (Vienna).
© Dominik Holzer

How can you consolidate such processes with the approach taken by Wolf Prix as the figurehead and main designer? His concepts typically seem to flow from hand sketches, and technology appears to play a minor role. How far does he get involved with technology, and how do you articulate the interface between a hand sketch or model and a sophisticated Rhino (or another tool) setup?

MP: It really depends at what stage you introduce your tools. You would be ill advised to start off your design using Digital Project. Such delivery-focused tools become relevant later on when key design decisions have been made already.

KS: When we start off a project using hand sketches, our typical process regards this sketch as a highly flexible reference. We then produce physical sketch models from that 2D reference. This step is not done by Wolf [Prix] himself but by individuals within a select group of trusted colleagues who can interpret his sketches. Those physical models become the essential reference for advancing the project even before we advance them using 3D digital tools. At the beginning we investigated ways to use computational tools to capture those physical models as they were, in order to grasp the freedom and veracity inherent to the original hand-sketch as much as possible. You only get that from physical models made by hand. We first used automated photogrammetry, then laser-scan technology, and now we use high-precision point cloud scanners and even AI. The technology keeps advancing, and we now have the required equipment in-house. This is an example of how we use technology early on.

Once we have captured the essence of the project digitally, we use the resulting information to advance the design in an iterative process, going back and forth between physical and digital models. The project never stays for long within one or the other medium. We need to advance it computationally to optimise geometric elements, but then take it back into the physical realm to verify at regular intervals.

Where does BIM sit with any of this?

KS: We are yet to come across a project that has to be delivered with BIM to the fullest extent. In a way, we have already been working with BIM methodology many years ago, and we were probably ahead of the pack implementing it; one could say we were too early as the rest of our collaborators were not able to contribute to our BIM efforts yet. In 2009, we set up the MOCAPE project with Digital Project but soon had to learn that other consultants and subcontractors were not able to contribute. Lyon was not a BIM project as such, but its organisation went according to BIM delivery mechanisms. The head contractor had to provide a 3D coordinator to assemble the 3D input from the various subcontractors. The required output was clearly articulated, and checking mechanisms were applied to coordinate the 3D input. Back then, neither the technology nor any of the local collaborators were sufficiently advanced BIM-wise.

▲ Figure 1.9

Musée des Confluences, Lyon, France (2001/2010–2014), façade panel installation, Coop Himmelb(l)au.
© Markus Pillhofer

KS: For some projects (e.g., the Central Bank Azerbaijan in Baku), we use Revit™ for the structural base-building in concrete but then use DP to generate the complex façade element. Revit could not have handled the geometric complexity of the hyperbolic shape.

PRACTICE INSERT: Coop Himmelb(l)au

MP: This concept of splitting responsibilities can extend into the way a project is organised; you could get a local [overseas] partner to look after the concrete shell, and we look after the façade and other complex shapes using different tools.

Are you comparing notes with your LA/London/other? Offices, and how do you collaborate with them when it comes to advancing and applying Design Technology?

KS: With exception of the LA office the design is typically generated locally and only leaves the Vienna headquarters once it is fairly advanced.

We embed key personnel from the main office at the local [site] office, either for a longer period or via periodic exchanges. When collaborating with local architects, we ensure that we work as one unified team and not as two offices. We never just share the 3D Master Design model; we always associate a dedicated person. Our LA office might be a bit different as we have been there more permanently than elsewhere (e.g., China).

What are the limitations of Design Technology use at Coop Himmelb(l)au? E.g., are there instances where Design Technology may obstruct rather than support great design?

KS: There are no limitations . . .

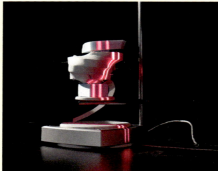

◀ Figure 1.10

PANEUM, House of Bread, Asten, Austria (2014–2017), 3D model and physical model scan.
© Coop Himmelb(l)au

◀ Figure 1.11

PANEUM, House of Bread, Asten, Austria (2014–2017), Coop Himmelb(l)au.
© Markus Pillhofer

How does Design Technology at Coop Himmelb(l)au evolve over time, and how do you respond to this challenge?

MP: One point is the adoption of specific BIM technology to fulfil the requirements of the market. Based on the type of large projects we do at Coop Himmelb(l)au, this rather practical step is expected of us. We will certainly investigate ways to transfer information from our early design studies as fluently into the 3D platform commonly used by our collaborators.

KS: On a more design-focused level, technology such as Mixed Reality shows particular promise. We need to get our head around its key benefits for us and understand where we can implement it most purposefully. When applying digital technology, we typically investigate this twofold: as part of the design and planning process and as part of fabrication/construction processes. We have come across examples where teams assemble and interrogate virtual 3D models jointly via Holo-lens or similar tools. One certainly could use this technology as part of morphological explorations on projects. Currently, we are also highly invested in the use of AI in the design process. Here, one strand of investigation also thematises the use of AI in the process of translation from the analogue to the digital realms.

1.3 Computational Design in Architecture Practice – A Brief History

How did the use of Design Technology evolve in practice since the first digital applications became commercially available? How did these applications get disseminated, and how has the continuous evolution of tools and technology infrastructure changed the landscape of architectural practice in the past forty to fifty years?

This section offers a historic perspective to the current use of Design Technology, thereby highlighting that its development is by no means over. In contrast, the application of Design Technology in architectural practice is ongoing, often coming in waves, depending on specific technical innovations or market constraints. When reflecting on the use of Design Technology over the decades, one specific aspect stands out: the key reasons and drivers for the earliest application of Design Technology in commercial practice in the 1960s are not too different from the reasons we use it today.

Design Technology – First Steps in Commercial Practice

When Ove Arup's team approached their design for the Sydney Opera House roof-structure in the late 1950s, they were faced with a major dilemma: the structure was so unusual and complex that traditional means of calculating it 'by hand' simply would have taken too long to yield any useful results. Not only was the project's morphology unprecedented, but it was also of a massive scale, requiring thousands of calculations and checks to conform to local guidelines and regulations. Arup hence leased a Ferranti Pegasus Mark 1 computer (the size of a room and located close to their London Headquarters) to advance the project. They needed to write their own software to analyse the structural behaviours of the roof (in a 1:60 model) and appropriate information for fabrication and construction, working together with researchers at Southampton University – who also owned a Pegasus machine.[2] Arup turned to Design Technology for two main reasons: firstly, to allow them to expand their existing design capabilities, and secondly to increase efficiencies in their work methods. To anyone associated with Design Technology nowadays, these two drivers still sound very familiar.

Arup's Opera House experiments are exemplar for several approaches in pushing the envelope of what was possible in design via the use of technological innovation and computing power. Given the major investment required to go down that path, it was prominently large firms that paved the way in the 1960s and 1970s, developing custom software applications to expand on their existing design capabilities.

Skidmore, Owings & Merrill (SOM) were among the earliest adopters when they formed their 'Computer Group' in 1964.[3] As a company with substantial history of working on large projects and embracing rationalisation and automation as part of their design approach, the use of computers to assist in the management of information related to functional and building-performance-related matters provided a perfect fit with their way of working. SOM counts among the pioneers in

---

2   Arup (1973) 'Sydney Opera House Special', in *The Arup Journal*, Vol. 8. No. 3, published by Ove Arup and Partnership, London, p. 10.
3   Lui, A. (2016) 'Data Dreams – The Computer Group and Architecture by Spreadsheet 1967–84', in *Drawing Futures, Speculations on Contemporary Drawing for Art and Architecture* (Allen L. and Pearson L.C., eds.), UCL Press (London), pp. 224–233. Available at: ucl.ac.uk/ucl-press

▲ Figure 1.12
Structural model test for the Sydney Opera House held at Southampton University.
© Henk Snoek/RIBA Collections

the advancement of software for architectural design purposes, developing their first Building Optimization Programme (BOP) in 1967, before any commercial CAD software became available. What followed were targeted efforts to develop custom applications for use on mainframe computers that would allow them to increase efficiencies in their documentation and test their design against several functional and performance-related criteria. Other large commercial architecture firms like HOK (Hellmuth, Obata and Kassabaum) soon established their own computing departments. The age of 'Computer Groups' and the inclusion of quantitative, calculus-heavy processes within large commercial design firms had begun.

Experimentation and Broader Appeal

One major milestone in the advancement of Design Technology in practice relates to custom applications that targeted specific building typologies via a set of object-oriented design data, linked to rule-based knowledge management systems. When the software application OXSYS[4] (Oxford Method) was developed in the late 1960s, it represented the first attempt to create a computational building design system to target specific construction methods – namely the design of hospital projects that followed strict UK regulations and guidelines. This idea was later picked up by Chuck Eastman in the United States on a much broader level. In the 1970s, Eastman helped develop a relational framework for the coordination of 2D/3D

---

4   The Oxford Method is described in the online archive of the Oxford Regional Hospital Board. Available at: https://archiveshub.jisc.ac.uk/data/gb160-h4/h4/13

building systems via a referring taxonomy and programming language. The goal of his research was to establish virtual building systems that would allow users to capture design and construction information in a standardised way. Eastman's work lay the foundations for what we would later consider BIM – Building Information Modelling and Digital Engineering. One of the earliest applications that became commercially viable was the Really Universal Computer-Aided Production System (RUCAPS™). Since the mid- to late 1970s, RUCAPS was applied by larger architecture practices on major reference projects around the world (such as Heathrow Terminal 3 in the mid-1980s). RUCAPS was quintessentially BIM. Despite the lack of network speed and connectivity across organisations, it nevertheless allowed users to work collaboratively via a mainframe hardware system.

Diversification in the PC Era

In contrast to custom software for mainframe computers up to that point, the standardised operating systems of PCs were ideal for software developers who could conceive tools for a mass market and at a much lower price point. In return, this resulted in the 'democratisation' of CAD skills, away from specialised operators towards common application by architects who may have had a few days' training. From the mid-1980s, 2D and 3D CAD tools like Bentley's Microstation™ or Autodesk's AutoCAD™ became the backbone of the documentation machinery in design practices around the world. Their inherent tool palette allowed application both for architecture as well as for engineering firms, making it possible for those two professions to share files and exchange data on their projects. Instead of relying entirely on marking up printed drawings and superimposing them via tracing, designers were given a chance to overlay and examine drawings digitally on the computer. Design and documentation software developers put emphasis on the ability of their tools to be not only customisable by their users but also expandable via dedicated plug-ins and custom scripts. As a result and in contrast to the dedicated 'computer' teams common in firms like SOM or HOK, individuals with little programming skills were now able to write subroutines to boost the efficiency of using CAD software.

From the mid-1980s and into the 1990s, limitations in computing power but also the lack of dedicated scripting skills seemed to diminish architects' appetite to fully explore what their digital tools could offer them. Only a small percentage of design firms put strong emphasis on developing custom plug-ins and scripts either to boost their design/documentation productivity or to allow

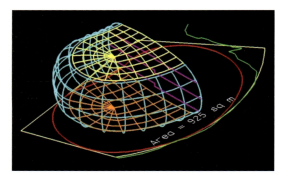 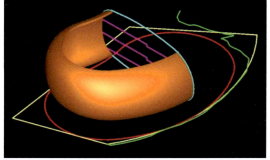

▲ Figure 1.13

Spherical segments on Chesa Futura.
© Foster + Partners

them to experiment with the CAD tool itself. By the mid-1990s, the most obvious push for Design Technology exploration focused on 3D visualisation.

3D Visuals to the Fore!

Many of the earliest Computer Aided Design Tools were programmed to work with three-dimensional data input that allowed users to produce perspective and isometric views of their design. In that sense, the software interface of the early commercial mainframe computer applications included basic wire frame design representations in 3D. As computers became more powerful, the wire frame aesthetic gave way to rendered surfaces with colour, reflection, and shadow definitions in three-dimensional space. At the start of the PC era in the early 1980s, such 'advanced' visuals provided an aesthetic that became synonymous with 'computer design' of its time. With the increasing computing power of the PC, the production of highly calculus-intensive 3D renders of projects came into the reach of practices who now did not have to rely any longer on highly spec'd Silicon Graphics machines. Advancements in graphics cards for PCs during the late 1980s and 1990s, hand in hand with improvements of rendering software, allowed architecture firms of any scale to produce detailed imagery of their projects.

Advances in raytracing/daylight simulation and texture-mapping pushed image quality in the vicinity of photorealism. Simultaneously, Adobe's raster graphics editor tool Photoshop™, which was first released to a mass-market in 1990, allowed designers to manipulate and re-edit their render output and achieve photorealistic representations of their project. Other vector graphics tools such as CorelDraw™ and Adobe's Illustrator™ emerged on the market at a similar time, with video editing tools soon to follow.

With architects using the increasing speed in rendering image stills to their advantage, they soon started expanding on their visualisation (Viz) efforts by producing animations of their projects in 3D. Here, the limitations of computing power of individual PCs represented a bottleneck in the production of visuals that was surmounted in the 2000s when render farms and online clusters/render farms helped to speed up the Viz process significantly. From a workflow perspective, the skills in geometry modelling, texture mapping, positioning of light sources, image/video production, screenplay, and editing advanced to the point where it could be seen as a separate technical expertise next to architectural design itself. In some instances, larger practices would outsource the production of high-end images and animations to third-party companies, which led to the emergence of dedicated visualisation firms in the early 2000s.

Geometric Exploration in Mainstream Practice

From the late-1990s, many architects started to experiment with the formal expression of their designs, using 3D modelling software. A growing pallet of free-form topographic modelling applications using non-uniform rational B-splines (NURBs) geometry in software applications, such as Alias | Wavefront Maya™ or McNeel's Rhinoceros™,[5] led design firms to push the boundaries of architectural geometry. Soon labelled 'Blob architecture', these practices

---

5   Available at: https://wiki.mcneel.com/rhino/rhinohistory

CHAPTER 1 Introduction – Defining Design Technology

proposed daring new designs driven by geometrical experimentation and at times underpinned by design theory that questioned the seemingly dogmatic constraints of the Cartesian coordinate system. As much as the opportunities for new geometric expressions seemed limitless on the computer screen, limitations of constructability and of construction material that catered for predominately orthogonal componentry became obvious.[6]

With the newly found freedom in exploring design geometry, an increasing number of design practices started searching for ways to make their daring concepts buildable by rationalising their morphology towards geometries that could be realised with the construction components/equipment available at the time. In doing so, they often applied architectural programming to inform their geometry subdivision and fabrication logic via computational scripts.[7] While Gehry predominantly opted for developable surfaces to approximate their façade design, projects at Foster + Partners were often advanced using translational surfaces or toroid segments.

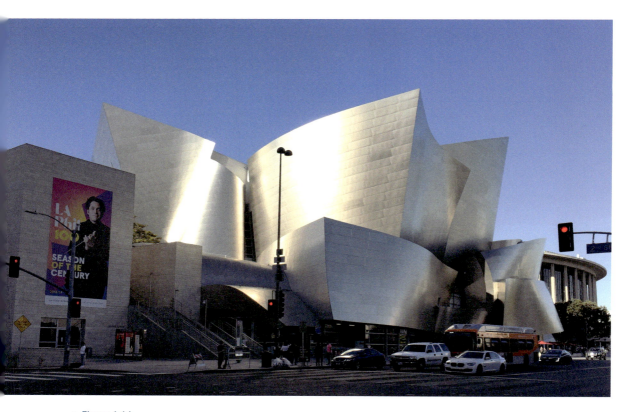

▲ Figure 1.14

Ruled surfaces used for the Disney Concert Hall façade by Frank Gehry, Los Angeles.
© Dominik Holzer

---

6   Leach, Neil (ed.) (2002) *Designing for a Digital World*, Wiley Academy, Hoboken, NJ.
7   Burry, M.C. (2011) *AD – Scripting Cultures: Architectural Design and Programming*, Wiley, Chichester.

▼ Figure 1.15
Mexico City Airport, parametric complex design form and concept to BIM.
© Foster + Partners

PRACTICE INSERT: Foster + Partners

As key representative of the high-tech architecture movement, Foster + Partners always had a technology-focused approach to their design. This clearly extends to their use of Design Technology and to an office setup that supports innovation and experimentation, paired with geometric exploration and computation. Under Hugh Whitehead, F+P's Specialist Modelling Group pioneered such efforts since the late 1990s, and they now work alongside the Applied Research and Development (ARD) group within the practice. ARD's Martha Tsigkari and Foster + Partners' former Project Architect Rafe Bertram reflect on the role of DT within the practice.

What role does Design Technology play at Foster + Partners? How do you implement it to support your distinctive design approach?

Martha Tsigkari (MT): Design Technology plays an integral role at Foster + Partners. Technology has always been thought of as a very important aspect of our approach to architecture, that goes hand in hand with our design sensitivities and the creativity within Foster + Partners. For the past fifty years, everybody has been pushing hard to use the latest methodology and the best tools for the job. That perception has not changed. For us it is all about how we can achieve our vision. Throughout the years, Foster + Partners has had a lot of innovative technologies applied in design. All of this comes together in a way that technology is not the foremost thing that you are looking at. The experience is the foremost thing that you are looking at! The fact that you are walking into a space, and it just feels right. What I find fascinating about the design output of our practice is that everything feels as it should be. Everything looks effortless. Things that I know have taken months and years to resolve, look exactly as they should, seemingly without trying. That is what makes the difference of a Foster + Partners building. In order to achieve that effortless look, you need to invest a lot of effort behind the scenes. We do not just design something we like, and then give it to the contractor to resolve. Our principle is: we will resolve every single detail, so we ensure that nothing looks out of place. To achieve that, you need to apply a lot of focused methodologies and strict pipelines. That is why technology is an intrinsic part of what we do.

On top of that, Design Technology is about how you liberate people [in the office] to understand better the repercussions of their design.

How does this unfold at Foster + Partners on a practical level?

MT: We use bespoke interactive applications that we have been developing for over a decade now to assist our performance-driven design process. These can

▼ Figure 1.16

Battersea Power Station, building morphology exploration.
© Foster + Partners

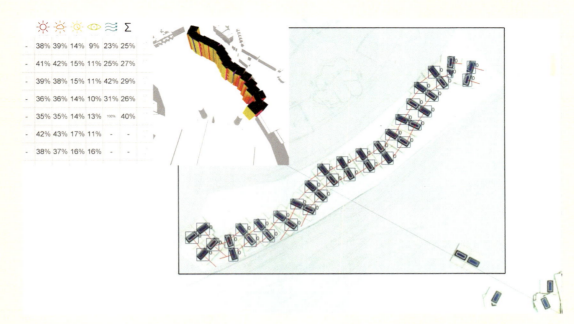

▲ Figure 1.16
(Continued)

operate on digital interfaces or even break down the barriers between physical and digital modelling. In that way, the designer can use an array of interfaces (from physical models and desktops to touch screens, tablets, or even AR or VR) to manipulate models in real time. During this process (which can be collaborative), key metrics, including daylight, insolation, wind, views, spatial connectivity, or even economic analytics, can be calculated on a linked digital model, allowing intuitive yet informed decision making early on in the design process.

How is Design Technology integrated at Foster + Partners on an organisational level?

MT: Currently we operate with six design studios, assisted by support groups across the practice. The support groups include the Applied Research and Development group (that I am part of), a Model Shop, a group focusing on Film and Visualisation, BIM, Workspace Consultancy, a Materials Research Centre (MRC), Communications, etc. All these offer a support network for the design studios.

▼ Figure 1.17

ARD team working across digital and analogue media.
© Foster + Partners

How do you decide the level of involvement of each group?

Martha: All these groups perform as internal consultancies but are part of the wider team. The involvement can vary and increase/decrease depending on different project phases and the foresight of the person who runs the project. When it comes to Design Technology, we have specialists like us in the Applied Research and Development (ARD) group, looking into anything in relation to R&D, innovation, Artificial Intelligence, optimisation, simulation, performance-driven design, interactive installations, complex geometry, design to production, augmented and Virtual Reality Additionally, we have designers spread across all Foster + Partner studios, who are technically versed. When I started here in 2006, we were ten staff who could program or operate using parametric design. Nowadays 20% of all staff within our design studios come with some level of parametric design or programming skills. Computational design is not foreign to them. On the contrary, these tools are in many cases adapted, applied, or even developed by the design studios.

Which management structures do you have in place to effectively apply Design Technology at Foster + Partners?

MT: One key management approach is embodied within our Design Review process. It is not a process set up to address technology per se; it is a process focused on design, which incorporates the use of technology. This is something that goes from a very small-scale review of a few people to a formal pinup of a project where our entire Design Board is involved in the discussion). It is important to note about Foster + Partners that we do not need anybody to police Design Technology because it is intrinsic to the way we think, and it has been for many years. We do not separate it; it is not something that needs to be imposed. Those working with me do not see me as a specialist person; we simply discuss design together and determine how we can move forward. We discuss ideas, and each party adds something to the equation.

Where does the Applied Research and Development (ARD) group sit in all of this? How do you operate?

MT: The ARD team currently consists of approximately ten staff; it was founded in 2012 as a spin-off from the Specialist Modelling Group at Foster + Partners. The team members typically have been at our practice for quite a while. We are a small unit, consisting of people who have either an architectural or engineering background (or both). Our common denominator is that we are all computer scientists in a way. We know how to program. If a Design Technology solution is not there yet, we will try to establish it. Therefore, we provide a mixed bag of support to the office. It started with complex geometry and design to production (which has been our bread and butter for many years), but it did spin off very quickly to many other areas, such as performance-driven design, interactive interfaces, optimisation, etc.

Are there any cultural clashes between Designers and Technology/ Technologists at Foster + Partners?

Rafe Bertram (RB): Cultural clashes? There are loads of clashes. It is probably a good thing. Tension always exists between the concentrated type thinking – of getting a scheme together and working on a computer in a super-zoned-in manner. The meditative and the collaborative. You need both. The only thing that begins to break that down is the speed of the iterative loops. The disadvantage of the meditative approach is that you might have good analysis, but you might not be getting all these diverse sets of inputs. The downside of the collaborative approach is that you might be talking lots but not basing it on anything well thought through.

The dream – and this is where the ARD team comes in so strongly – is a way of working that enables a collaborative format while quickly feeding in the meditative inputs.

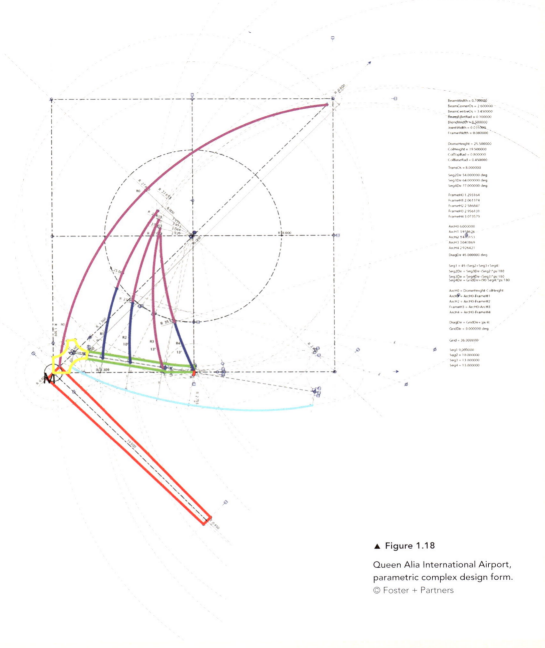

▲ **Figure 1.18**

Queen Alia International Airport, parametric complex design form.
© Foster + Partners

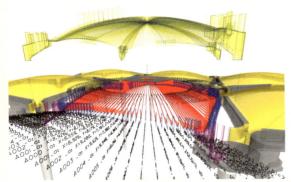

MT: When you have one of our lead designers talking about not the tension between architects and technologists but basically the tension between a physical and a virtual model and how we can map the two together, then you realise where we are as a company. I do not think Rafe sees me as a technologist; he sees me as a collaborator. Our common goal is to materialise our vision of experience and space we want to produce. All these are based on the discussion we are having about how we collaborate better using technology. The tensions we are having are tensions that have to do with better uses of technology rather than . . . whether we need to use technology in the first place.

Does the Applied Research + Development Group operate as a standalone (support) team, or is it integrated across projects?

MT: It is a mix of the two, particularly because our research component springs from needs that we have identified or the strategic vision that we have in place. This has usually a three-to-five-year horizon and looks into what are potential new technologies and capabilities that we can take hold of and put in the hands of the architects now? We are generally very proactive in terms of the research we undertake. We'll find an interesting solution, which then becomes a tool, a process, or a pipeline that can be used throughout the office. We also investigate more strategic, long-term research, and we are seeking collaboration with universities and peers in the industry (particularly in construction) in doing that.

The way we interact with project teams has changed a lot since I started at Foster + Partners. When computational design came along, programming/parametrics – whatever you want to call it – someone like me started from a position of being regarded as a magician: 'Go there, do your magic, and solve our problem . . .'. You ended up being a firefighter. By now, people have realised the difference we can make to the success of the project. Because of how technology evolved, how we as the ARD evolved, and the way the office keeps evolving, we now get introduced on projects from an early stage.

At Foster + Partners, is technology just a means to an end, is it a major driver of innovation and creativity, or somewhere in between?

RB: I do not see Design and Technology as being very different. We are after an architecture that is born out of problems and opportunities, and spirit and dream, and reality. It is an architecture that is born out of a multiplicity of needs. Some of those needs can be expressed openly in a spiritual dreamy way, and some of those needs have to be expressed in an incredibly scientific rigorous and analytically researched way.

There is a spectrum in between. If one takes that as a belief, in design you need processes, tools, or methodologies to allow different inputs to inform design. Some of them will depend on multidisciplinary analytical tools, and others will need a walk in the park!

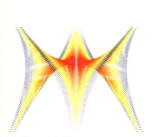

▲ Figure 1.19

Morphology, Molteni ARC table analysis.
© Foster + Partners

▲ Figure 1.20

Morphology, Molteni ARC table finished design.
© Molteni&C

In terms of tool use – how are you facilitating the transition from your Rhino/scripting/C-sharp/parametric-modelling-focused approach by designers to your delivery in Revit?

MT: That is a straightforward question to answer: In collaboration with our BIM team, we have been working on particular processes that facilitate transition between platforms. We are not stuck in any specific platform, but we will use whatever does the job best. We facilitate very fast translation of data from one platform to the other. In doing that, not only have we devised particular workflows, we have also devised our own tools (for instance, we have Hermes, our own version of Flux, developed in-house). We are also particularly interested in promoting the idea of global, open schema that we can use not only at Foster + Partners but also throughout the industry. IFC is currently one such format, but we support anything that has to do with a simple, open global standard that we can use industry wise.

Back to the basics, 1,300 people globally – how are they distributed across all your offices globally?

MT: We have our headquarters here in London, spread across number of buildings. We centralised the services we offer, and therefore it is crucial to have a dissemination and collaboration strategy in place that is common for all the offices globally. We are all working in the same way, have the same tools, use the same processes, and everybody can use them.

What are the limitations of Design Technology use at Foster + Partners?

MT: We do not think in terms of limitations; we think in terms of possibilities. I cannot think about things that limit us.

RB: What the technology has not yet done yet is to be as accessible as a magnet and a stack of paper. It has huge advantages in many other ways, and therefore I bring up the culture of the design review. Being able to match the best points of that type of design review is the challenge that I can see. Watch this space because we are on it. . . . That is a limitation. There is an opportunity for a consistently adopted, multidisciplinary, multiplayer design and analysis interactive tool.

▼ Figure 1.21
ARD team using Hololens technology for urban exploration.
© Foster + Partners

MT: I find the answer very interesting because I am thinking about this question in terms of, 'What can we not do with technology?' From that perspective, I see the immense opportunities we have created. Now that I hear Rafe's perspective – he is talking about tools and applications we already developed to an extent. I understand how differently we think about this. I am co-heading the digital innovation group in the office. One of the initiatives we have as a group was about how to modernise our design board reviews. How do we take interactive design reviews to the next level with technology support? We went through a big exercise to find the appropriate software and hardware to facilitate this. We are in the process of having a much more adaptable way of working (remotely worldwide). This is in the pipeline. Of course, we are not there yet. That simplicity [Rafe is looking for] is not something that you are going to get from one day to another.

Are there instances where Design Technology may obstruct rather than support great design?

RB: I think so, it can do that. There is a nice flow which is a psychological state of mind where you lose track of time. When you are so deep in a discussion, in playing with a toy (as a kid), or you are making something. It is hard to create technologies that are compatible with flow. I am lucky enough to be working with the ARD and other teams as they allow me a glimpse of what that flow feels like. A Design Technology–enabled flow. That is amazing . . . and rare. When things work perfectly and you have that flow, it is a great thing. Sketching on a piece of trace with a lead pencil allows for this flow, the more complex, [technically] empowered, and enabled the design process is, the more could go wrong.

◀ Figure 1.22

ARD team exploring the use of onsite robotics.
© Foster + Partners

How does Design Technology at Foster + Partners evolve over time, and how does the practice respond to this challenge?

MT: Design Technology evolves in terms of the opportunities that are given to us, based on technological advances but also in terms of strategic aspirations that we have. These two do not always come hand in hand. For example, ARD started looking into AR and VR almost twenty years ago. We collaborated with University College London to develop ARTHUR, an Augmented Reality research project that allowed for full, multi-user design in Augmented Reality – although the kit at the time cost $100K per person. But because we investigated the possibilities of this technology so many years ago, today we can use AR and VR not so much as a visualisation tool but as a design collaboration tool at a fraction of the price. What lies in our future in terms of DT is twofold: it must align with what we feel is strategically important but also with what is available. As a company, we are good at making unavailable things available. That is what puts us in a very good position within the industry in terms of R&D.

1.4 The Proliferation of Parametric Design and Scripting

As highlighted by the example of Foster + Partners, a major shift in the way practices engage digital tools as part of their design process occurred around 2000 with the introduction of parametric design applications to a mass market. The playful pushing and pulling of surface geometry in 3DsMax™, Maya, or Rhino gave way to a more structured and controlled way of managing geometric and non-geometric relations that drive the morphology of architecture projects.[8] Ever since Gehry's 1992 Barcelona Fish Sculpture (which was conceived using the digital design and manufacturing tool CATIA™), the proliferation of parametric design into design and engineering practice was unstoppable. With CATIA requiring a substantial time and money investment, easily accessible alternatives such as Bentley's Generative Components™ and later McNeel's Explicit History (later renamed Grasshopper) offer computational support that complements open-ended and highly iterative design and tie into exploratory design processes via rule-based and generative approaches. They give architects the ability to evaluate many options with a high degree of complexity in a short amount of time.

In that vein, parametric techniques are strongly aligned with conceptual thinking and intuitive design exploration applied by architects.[9] Instead of generating geometry via precise Cartesian coordinates input (which implies a level of determination about the modelling intent), designers rather set up relationships and rules that govern form and structure. In addition, the use of generative algorithms within such flexible setups allows designers to include optimisation routines for form finding or spatial layout, thereby introducing novel palettes to the architect's toolkit. From 2010, a great number of design practices started to take advantage of these optimisation routines, as they were easily accessible via plug-ins to their existing drafting software. Whereas the need for expert skills made it difficult for 'scripting' to proliferate across mainstream practice, these pre-configured optimisation routines available in Grasshopper lowered the barriers for design firms to engage with complex problem solving.

By the mid-2010s, Grasshopper had become the de facto standard application for parametric modelling for architecture practices. The flexibility inherent to rule-based modelling enabled through visual scripting suits the typical design approach by architects where things move fast, and many options need to be scrutinised in a short period of time. As a side effect, the combination of parametric design alterations informed by building physics performance feedback informs the architect/engineer dialogue and allows those engineering firms who embrace the parametric workflow to deploy their knowledge more directly on projects.

In 2003, initially focusing heavily on the use of Bentley's Generative Components, a group of Design Technology leaders in practice joined forces with academic researchers to form the Smartgeometry group.[10] Whoever wanted to learn about the latest and greatest in parametric design would

---

8 See also at: Spiller, N. (2008) *Digital Architecture Now: A Global Survey of Emerging Talent*, Thames & Hudson, London.

9 Aish, R. (1981) 'CAD Support for Intuitive and Strategic Design Thinking', in *Colofon*, VCA Mededelingen, Amsterdam.

10 Available at: www.archdaily.com/398406/practice-2-0-10-years-of-smart-geometry

▲ Figure 1.23

Prototypes at the Smartgeometry Workshop and Conference at IAAC (Barcelona) in 2010.
© Dominik Holzer

join their (initially) annual workshops and associated conference, held in major cities around the world. Over the years, Smartgeometry has evolved to become platform-agnostic, with conferences and workshops occurring every second year. The Smartgeometry workshops later shifted from a predominantly parametric-design-focused software experimentation and geometry rationalisation events to more physical model- making and prototyping, informed by a broad range of physical (or other) constraints. Since the early days of Smartgeometry, other events and groups have emerged, where leading design practices investigate the use of Design Technology to advance their design capability jointly with academics in the field: Advances in Architectural Geometry (2008),[11] the Design Modelling Symposium (2008),[12] or Fabricate (2011),[13] just to name a few. One aspect that all these events have in common is an opportunity to showcase the latest developments in Design Technology and provide representatives from practice and academia alike an opportunity to try out something new (outside the pressures of everyday project delivery).

1.5 Object-oriented Design Documentation Going Mainstream

While topology-based modelling tools were used extensively for geometric exploration since the early 1990s, firms were looking for ways to introduce greater efficiency in their documentation and design-coordination processes. Until the new millennium, the predominant technology supporting design documentation was the use of 2D CAD tools. Design firms were looking for alternatives that would allow them to introduce greater efficiencies into their documentation process, in particular by linking the production of documentation sets to 3D models, where changes only had to be carried out once and would then automatically update the associated plan/section/elevation drawings.

Bespoke applications for object-oriented Virtual Building Design started to emerge, such as Graphisoft's ArchiCAD™ (1987) and Charles River Software's Revit (1997), which was later bought by Autodesk. Bentley worked

---

11 Available at: www.architecturalgeometry.org/aag18/about/
12 Available at: https://design-modelling-symposium.de/about/archive/
13 Available at: www.fabricate.org/

on BIM integration in their 2D Microstation platform via the Triforma™ tool bench. BIM-enabled documentation by architects has seen major uptake globally from about 2005 onward with tools becoming increasingly sophisticated. Initially focusing mainly on introducing greater efficiencies in documentation-related activities, the features of BIM tools soon expanded into 3D coordination of BIMs from multiple stakeholders, 4D construction sequencing for contractors, 5D cost management for quantity surveyors, and 6D linking of design/construction models to facility and asset management processes. A comprehensive summary of the emergence of BIM and its proliferation into different streams of inquiry can be found in the *BIM Handbook* by Eastman et al.[14]

Fifteen years after its broader adoption commenced in architectural practice, the advancement and proliferation of BIM are still evolving. BIM has now become the de facto 'best-practice' approach for the coordinated and structured delivery of most major construction projects in the world. The diversification of BIM into different fields of inquiry pushes architecture firms to reconsider the way they exchange design information with their project partners, including the client. The associated productivity gains across the entire construction sector are currently being addressed by government departments around the world who promote the use of 'life cycle' BIM via local policies; this results in legal and procedural ramifications for typical BIM workflows to be considered by the supply chain.

1.6   Digital Models for Structural and Environmental Performance Feedback

In parallel with object-oriented design and documentation, another field of inquiry emerged within the broader context of Design Technology: building physics analysis and simulations. Since the 1970s tools have been developed to help designers understand the implications of structural and climatic conditions on their design and optimise physical building performance.

Pairing structural analysis with flexible computational modelling (as facilitated by parametric design) has the advantage of allowing designers to test the physical performance of their designs under different geometric configurations without the need for tedious remodelling and (re)association of base conditions. This facilitates a workflow that speeds up the testing of design alternatives while allowing the designers to conduct preliminary structural trend analysis in the earlier design stages. Data interfaces (schemers) communicate between tools and help to automate the information-flow between geometry generation and simulation. Numerous applications interfacing with McNeel's Rhino modelling tool (e.g., Kangaroo, Karamba, Kiwi or Robot) allow for this workflow to unfold.

Early approaches for CAD supporting environmental analysis date back to experiments undertaken by Tom Maver and his colleagues at the ABACUS[15] group at the University of Strathclyde in the late 1970s and early

---

14 Eastman, C., Teicholz, P., Sacks, R. and Liston, K. (2008) *BIM Handbook, A Guide to Building Information Modeling for Owners, Managers, Designers, Engineers, and Contractors*, John Wiley & Sons, Hoboken, NJ.

15 Maver, T.W., Smith, M., Watts, J. and Aish, R. (1979) 'Implications for Practice and Education', *Proceedings of PArC 79*, Berlin, pp. 221–232.

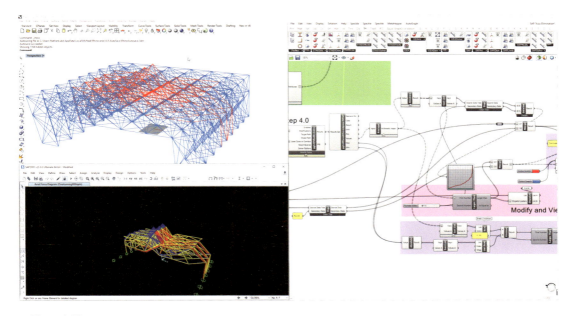

▲ Figure 1.24

Automating the interface between parametric modelling and structural analysis in SAP2000.
© Geometry Gym

1980s. Back then, large architecture firms would typically write their own software to carry out environmental analysis, covering a limited set of bespoke criteria.

The 'engineering backbone' of many commercial applications that for solar/daylight analysis and heat gain was facilitated by the freely available energy simulation engine DOE-2.[16] Produced by the U.S. Department of Energy, it was later advanced into EnergyPlus™, which has remained the benchmark application in this field to the present day. EnergyPlus connects with a broad range of third-party tools in order to allow designers to determine a diverse spectrum of environmental factors, including energy consumption for heating and cooling, ventilation, lighting, and water use in buildings. With increasing computing power, highly-calculus-intensive software for simulating airflow in the form of computational fluid dynamics (CFD) saw its uptake in (engineering) practice from the late 1990s. It allowed designers not only to test the solar impact on their design but to consider human comfort levels and structural integrity under different wind/weather conditions.

A major development in integrating environmental analysis as part of conceptual design occurred around 2010. Applications entered the market that allowed architects to connect their parametric 3D models with building physics evaluation (particularly in Grasshopper). Tools such as Geco™

---

16 Winkelmann, F.C., Birdsall, B.E., Buhl, W.F., Ellington, K.L., Erdem, A.E., Hirsch, J.J. and Gates, S. (1993) *DOE – 2 Supplement, Version 2.1E*, Lawrence Berkeley National Laboratory, Springfield.

(which linked Grasshopper to Ecotect™), Diva™, and ultimately Ladybug/Honeybee found widespread adoption in design practice by assisting architects to test a variety of environmental performance issues in their designs. In recent years, those analysis tools, which connect directly to parametric design modelling and morphology exploration, have seen uptake by designers. Launched in 2012, the solar analysis application Ladybug (which forms part of the Rhino/Grasshopper family of tools) allows designers to intuitively test design options in close to real time via parametric geometry variations.[17] Results can get displayed via clearly readable colour charts that are mapped onto the underlying geometry or via other types of numeric output. This helps architects to better understand the underlying environmental trends associated with their design decisions, and a broad range of auxiliary tools now complement its initial focus on shading, solar gain, wind, and thermal comfort.

Many of the technologies mentioned in this chapter have a fundamental impact on how design firms operate and how information flows within their project teams. The Bjarke Ingels Group (BIG) has a group of computational design specialists within their ranks, who help push the strong design agenda via the use of latest tools for analysis, visualisation, and delivery of their projects.

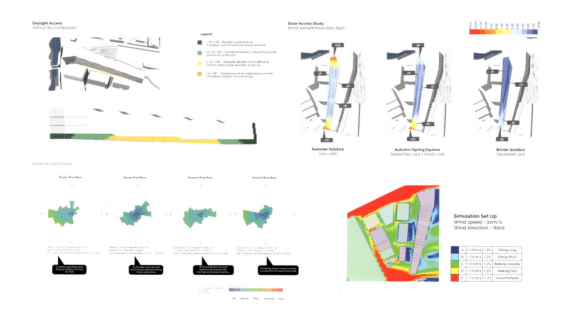

▲ Figure 1.25

KGX solar access and CFD wind analysis.
© Heatherwick Studio

---

17 Aksin, F.N. and Arslan Selçuk, S. (2021) 'Use of Simulation Techniques and Optimization Tools for Daylight, Energy and Thermal Performance – The Case of Office Module(s) in Different Climates', *Proceedings of the 39th eCAADe Conference – Vol 2*, University of Novi Sad, Novi Sad, Serbia, 8–10 September 2021, pp. 409–418.

The following pages highlight their unique approach to the integration of Design Technology within several of their studios.

Their feedback will be followed by Chapter 2. It explores how organisations can adjust their work methods and their office structure to maximise the benefits they derive from Design Technology. The chapter discusses the often-times ambivalent relationship between designer and technology, to then address ways to align culture with technological support.

► **Figure 1.26**

BIG Ideas, examples of annual yearbooks.
© Dominik Holzer

BIG (BJARKE INGELS GROUP)

PRACTICE INSERT: BIG - Bjarke Ingels Group

The Bjarke Ingels Group (BIG) is a young practice that has seen a stellar rise on the global architecture scene since their foundation in 2001. Technology does not appear to be in the foreground of their design process, yet their 'sculpting' approach to architectural design often relies on strong Design Technology support and staff who introduce technological innovation to help realise their ambitious projects. Big Ideas is such a group within the firm and their excellence in the field has expanded via their global network of studios in recent years. Among other tasks, they complement BIG's design morphology with environmental (and other) performance feedback). Computational Designer Oliver Thomas from their NYC office draws a comprehensive picture of BIG's current Design Technology efforts and future aspirations.

What role does Design Technology play, and how do you implement it to support BIG's distinctive design approach?

Oliver Thomas (OT): BIG is first and foremost a design firm, and this provides a very natural filter for what technologies do work and what technologies do not work. Especially on these high pace projects. The role of Design Technology at BIG covers three main aspects:

How can we use computational tools to enhance the design itself or enhance the design process, purely from a design perspective?

Secondly, there is a role of Design Technology in the design process more from a production standpoint: how can we streamline the production? This could be something as simple as . . . how can we utilise tools to free up time; like a simple script that places thousands of trees? Will that save a designer a couple of evenings, so that we can spend more time in critical design and design thinking (which is where we do our best work)?

And thirdly, there's also a communication aspect: how can technology allow us to communicate our designs clearly. Whether this refers to visualisation, animation, virtual reality, or Augmented Reality, this is about all tools we use to communicate our stories and our ideas. Augmented Reality (AR) and Virtual Reality (VR) are particularly new to the practice; they are giving us a new bandwidth of communication. It is very much about how we can support and enhance the unique design process of BIG. Because of that, we are always testing new tools and new plug-ins.

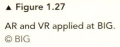

▲ Figure 1.27

AR and VR applied at BIG.
© BIG

With VR and AR, has that seen a special push now that COVID has restricted access to physical model making and working with physical models?

OT: Yes, it has clearly been given a boost, particularly the VR. We have partnered with a firm called Spaceform, who offer a virtual meeting room where you can pin up stuff in a virtual space and curate 3D virtual models. COVID has expedited that experiment and that technology itself; there are a few projects where everyone in the meeting has a headset on and they are meeting in virtual reality because we cannot meet physically. Physical models remain very important, we are still building models and sending them to clients. VR definitely has not replaced physical models, but they are expanding our communication capabilities and the bandwidth of communication. We now know that we do not need to travel as much for meetings, we only need to do one or two; we can cover collaboration virtually if we have to. I think it is just a confirmation that we can now do these things. I would have questioned whether any large architecture firm can work remotely. Now we have proven that we can.

How is Design Technology integrated at a BIG on an organisational level?

OT: Copenhagen and New York are the two offices that developed the DT side very quickly. Historically, Copenhagen has always had a very strong global simulation department, run from under the BIG Ideas umbrella. In the NYC office, computation in early stages was done on an ad hoc basis inside the teams through smart staffing, then extended into the later stages with help from the BIM team. Now with two full-time computational specialists in NYC, we can further bridge into all reaches of the project and process.

We work with specialist groups (whether it is BIM, computation, or visualisation) as in-house consultants. It is more of an empowering approach where we train up the designers and help them get to a level where they can implement these tools in the design process themselves, to a certain extent. In that sense, it is not like us being a specialist department and the designers throw us problem for us to fix (even though this can still be the case sometimes). The BIM team is teaching the design team how to use Revit and how to use BIM. The visualisation team is teaching them how to use Enscape and V-Ray. As DT specialists, we will tackle some of the more advanced workflows, but it is about elevating the designers and their skills. We still do not have an overall Design Technology [leader] figure acting across all our offices, although that is something we are investigating currently. The London office is a lot bigger now. We are about seventy people approximately, and then also, we open the Barcelona office with about twenty or thirty people.

▼ Figures 1.28

Examples of different types of BIM work at BIG.
© BIG

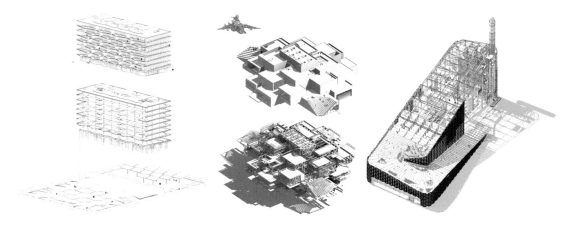

The BIM group is like an in-house consultancy, but it is not necessarily run by any of the partners. It is just who would someone like Jan report to?

OT: We report directly to our CEO. She is great, and she understands the power of BIM. There are partner groups that are looking at technology firm-wide, and we formed groups called BIG BIT and BIG Compute, where we discuss and test technology in the office. It consists of people from the BIM team, the computational team, the Visualisation team, and a couple of part-ners, and we discussed technology in general. Those sessions are slightly more informal.

Which management structures do you have in place to effectively apply Design Technology at BIG?

OT: There are a formal and an informal side to it. Formally the office is split into two sides, Ops and LEAD (landscape, engineering, architecture, and planning), and as technology specialists we often straddle the line between the two, but for the most part we are part of the LEAP side of things. Then we have separate specialist teams, BIM, Computation, Viz and the model shop, etc., and from there we disseminate technology, workflows, guides into the teams. We do also have informal project roles of BIM Leads or Computational leads where someone from the team who has a particular interest in that side of thing steps up and takes responsibilities for tasks in the team and the project. On the other hand, infor-mally, everyone in the office is aware of the teams and individuals whom they can approach for a specific problem, and they can come and ask for help on specific ad hoc tasks on the project.

How do your Design Technology experts interact with the project teams? Where do you fit in a project? Are you costed towards projects or an overhead budget?

OT: It is fifty-fifty give or take. Especially on the BIM side, I am assigned to a group of projects, and I will see a project through from sketch design to design development (or whatever the design stage). On that level, you are working with one foot in the team, and as far as I am aware that billing is on the project. You meet with the team regularly, and in some cases, you take responsibility for a portion of the projects. Often that relates to an advanced workflow for the façade or something along those lines. On the other side, you have more informal approaches where we are asked to support with a quick exercise or a script, or questions like: 'Hey, can we do this in AR or VR on this project'. It could be anything from the concept stage to the later stages. That level of support is provided more informally, depending on what we are doing and how much time it takes. There is a level above where we are testing tools. It is important to always be experimenting with new tools and advancing our own skill sets. Some people in the office are interested in the Unreal game engine, for example, but also even within the BIM/Computation team, each person has their own area of expertise and interests. There is a little bit of R&D time dedicated to making sure we always keep an eye on the horizon of what is coming. In Copenhagen, there is slightly different dynamic, as there you have different roles via their distinction between the constructing architects and the design architects.

How does your provision of support typically play out?

OT: It can completely depend on the skill set of the team you are working with. If someone has a problem and they are brand new to Grasshopper, I am totally game to sit down and teach them some stuff. But equally, if they need something

PRACTICE INSERT: BIG - Bjarke Ingels Group

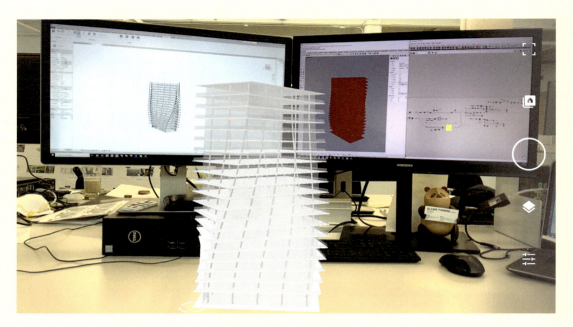

▲ Figure 1.29

Mixed reality applied at BIG.
© BIG

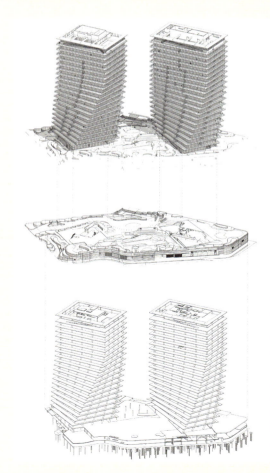

◀ Figure 1.30

Example of BIM work at BIG.
© BIG

done by tomorrow, then you have to quickly fix things yourself. It can happen in any design stage. Most of my work (because I am still in the BIM team) is in the slightly latest stages of SD and beyond, because that is where we implement them the most, but the point of providing computational design support can vary. It is mostly in the earliest stages, but it can also occur later on.

How does the transition from design to delivery processes occur at BIG? What is the current suite of options that you are working with to accomplish this?

OT: We have a very clear design tool, which is Rhino and Grasshopper, and a documentation tool, which is Revit and Dynamo™. Like many firms, we were battling with an interoperability issue. We were playing around with all the plug-ins one can imagine, whether it was Flux at the time or Speckle more recently. Then Rhino Inside came about, which fits well within my skill sets because I have a Rhino and Grasshopper background, as well as being a BIM specialist. Rhino Inside has been a bit of a game changer for us in the transition from design into documentation. Designers and the computational guys in Grasshopper are starting to come over into the BIM world because they can extend their design process directly into the documentation process. We also see more 'BIM typical' architects, who are interested in the Grasshopper and Rhino world because now they can come into it from the Revit more comfortably. We are seeing the lines blurred for sure with this tool.

How do you collaborate across offices?

OT: The BIG offices work semi-regionally. The New York office looks after the Americas and also South America; Copenhagen does most of Europe and Asia, London does the UK in the Middle East, etc. The projects do not overlap much, and we will share resources between the studios on occasion. In the New York office, we have a BIM team, and in the Copenhagen office, we have one as well. We also have a computational specialist in New York (as part of the BIG Ideas umbrella) who liaises with his counterparts on Copenhagen regularly. They have weekly meetings for the visualisation team and so forth. Within the offices, collaboration can occur in an organic way. What we are currently pushing is communication of different technologies between the offices and sharing the associated resources.

We try and pull in the characters, whether they are from the BIM team or the competition team, or anyone dealing with a particular topic. Another way that we are trying to spread information (which COVID has amplified) is represented via what we call 'Big Schools' and 'BIG Academies'. BIG Schools is an interesting part of BIG where people in the office who might have specialty knowledge in anything (it could be Design Technology or Fire Safety) share some of their own knowledge in a presentation. It is a great way to share information. That appears to be a struggle for many architecture firms: how can you spread knowledge across an organisation?

Are there any potential limitations associated to your Design Technology use at BIG?

OT: Because of the speed and the scope of products, one limitation is a potential natural filter to some technologies regarding whether that technology is implementable now, or if it is something that we will keep an eye on for the future. That is one area where the unique environment of BIG has its pros and cons. One limitation for the spread of DT use is the speed and scope of projects, specifically because we are a design firm. One other thing – it is not really a limitation – but we always need to educate staff and overcome stigmas that are sometimes associated with technologies. You say the words 'parametric', 'Grasshopper', or 'computation', and people immediately think crazy design. This is nothing unique to BIG, it is an industry-wide thing. Sometimes colleagues are surprised that we suggest using certain tools simply because it is going to save them time. There is a whole other side to it of becoming a more efficient architect and streamlining/automating things.

Where would you like to take things with Design Technology at BIG?

OT: The key thing for me is about continually integrating it into our workflows and staying up to date. There is still a lot that we can improve on, even at a firm like BIG, which is already very technology integrated. There's always room for improvement. I am passionate about making the individual designers at BIG more computationally fluent in whatever they are interested in. As architects, we are one of the faster ones in the AEC industry, but we are slow adopters of technology in general in our sector. Technology is not a silver bullet to resolve this, but it is definitely a huge piece of the puzzle. I am interested in talking about technology within BIG, with other practices within the industry. How can we make BIGsters more computationally BIM and visualisation fluid? But then also as an industry: how can we increase conversations around technology and maybe use a little flavour of entrepreneurship as well? Architects should become a bit more entrepreneurial.

▼ Figure 1.31

View of the BIG NYC office.
© Max Touhey

Chapter 2

Positioning Technology Within Design Practice

Design Technology is about much more than the provision of tool and infrastructure support for architects. Due to its progressing expansion, it now affects many aspects of design practice, and it has become closely tied to the way design firms operate. Chapter 2 offers a critical reflection on the use of Design Technology to offer a 'best fit' for any organisation. One thing becomes clear: there is no one singular or even 'best' way to achieve this. Instead, firms need to be aware of the factors that influence their Design Technology setup across the different activities they pursue.

2.1 The Ambivalent Relationship Between Architects and (Design) Technology

To position the application of Design Technology in contemporary practice, it is essential to consider the wider cultural context of architectural design and technology. Choices architects make regarding their uptake of design tools and related infrastructure depend by nature on their intrinsic approach to architectural design and associated processes. Those who perceive architectural design predominantly as the creative act of advancing ideas via deliberation and sketching might see technology as a necessary evil. Others, who openly embrace technology as a key driver of architectural innovation, might welcome it as an essential feature in their tool palette. There is no fixed rule on how this is approached in practice. Is design truly creative only when it flows from the designer's imagination to pen and paper? Is the strength of a concept automatically weakened if it is influenced by auxiliary input/tools? The schism between creative and analytical design is not new, and the way Design Technology is positioned in different firms typically responds directly to the philosophy of their leaders.

The relation between technology and design practice has been going through highs and lows over the decades and centuries. It has equally been embraced with excitement and admiration as it has been dismissed and shunned as something that distracts from the 'purity' of design. If Renaissance masters like Da Vinci and Brunelleschi were lauded for their ability to combine artistic genius with technical inventiveness, following styles such as the Baroque focused predominantly in their aesthetic design approaches, the visual appeal of their work by far outweighed technological advance.

The first industrial revolution, hand in hand with the rise of the engineering professions, furthered the rift between design as an artistic process and technology as its analytical sideshow.[1] Against the backdrop of the industrial revolution,

---

1 In many countries, a division between 'Design Architect' and 'Technical Architect' has been introduced that persists until today.

John Ruskin provided a sharp critique on the dehumanising effects of technological advance on society. Ruskin fundamentally questioned the human's potential to handle the extension of their abilities via technical means and warned about the *contrast between the advanced technology of the doing and the questionable nature of what is being done.*[2] As much as some of Ruskin's suspicions on the effects of technology on human nature bordered on technophobia, his warning on the distractive capability of technology from observing and doing still resonates with designers and those implementing Design Technology alike.

During stylistic periods associated to Neo-Classicism, Neo-Gothic, or Art Nouveau, architectural practices (apart from a few exceptions) were often relegated as decorators, leaving it to the engineer to break new ground on grand civil projects.

Technology in Practice – From the Modernist Movement to Digital Architecture

It comes as no surprise that many of the most influential projects Le Corbusier references in his Modernist manifesto *Toward an Architecture*[3] (*Vers une architecture)* are in fact engineering projects. The radical shift of the Modernism movement away from architecture as a decorative art firmly embraced innovation and technological advance as one of the key drivers of architectural creativity. At the same time, the rationalism inherent to the Modern style, hand in hand with its increased use of standardised building systems and components, radically changed the architects' interaction with the supply chain of building componentry, as well as their dialogue with collaborating engineers. Even more so, it changed the nature of the architect's interaction with the builder. Kenneth Frampton discusses this in greater detail in reference to the Bauhaus movement.[4]

Many of the figureheads of the Modernist era are lauded for their craft-based approach and close collaboration with builders and manufacturers, as exemplified by the aluminium façade detailing of Pierre Chareau's *Maison de Verre* in Paris or Mies van der Rohe's exposed cruciform pillars at the Villa Tugendhat in Brno. The irony related to these early masterpieces is the simultaneous drive of the Modernist masters towards buildings that can be assembled using mass-produced and standardised componentry, with a strong focus on functional aspects of their projects. In retrospect, a key legacy left by the Modernist movement (perverted by doctrines of Rationalism, Behaviourism, and Pragmatism)[5] was an increased detachment of architects from a personal engagement with the client and the builder.[6] Across construction industries globally, the decades after the Second World War are characterised by the rise of the head contractor, hand in hand with the emergence of ever more specialised trades that focus on small portions of work. The progressing segregation of professions in the construction industry since the 1950s has led to redistribution of roles and responsibilities in an ever more information-rich sector.[7] Unable to cope with the sheer volume of

---

2   Davis, A. (2015) *Part II: Technology, The Cambridge Companion to John Ruskin*, edited by Francis O'Gorman, Cambridge University Press, Cambridge, p. 172.
3   Le Corbusier (1924) *Vers une Architecture*, 2nd ed., G. Crès, Paris.
4   Frampton, K. (1980) *Modern Architecture: A Critical History*, Thames & Hudson, London, p. 184.
5   Jencks, C. (1977) *The Language of Post-Modern Architecture*, Academy Editions, London, p. 10.
6   MacEwen, M. (1974) *Crisis in Architecture*, RIBA Publications, London.
7   Taylor, J. and Levitt, R.E. (2004) 'Understanding and Managing Systemic Innovation in Project-based Industries', in *Innovations: Project Management Research*, edited by D. Cleland, J. Pinto and D. Slevin, Project Management Institute, Pennsylvania, pp. 83–99.

information to process across multiple stakeholders and ill-equipped to manage the financial aspects of project coordination on larger projects, architects further offloaded responsibilities to project managers.

As the Modernist style evolved during several decades of strong economic growth and prosperity in the 1960s–1980s, new styles emerged. They respond, each in their own way, to the Modernist movement, and their key characteristics influence how Design Technology gets positioned in some of the world's leading practices today. On one end of the spectrum, the High-tech movement spearheaded by architects like Norman Foster, Nicholas Grimshaw, and Richard Rogers searched to expand the vocabulary of modernist architecture via technological advances that offer greater freedom and flexibility in design. With glass, concrete, and steel as the predominant construction materials, novel solutions were found for structural systems and façade components, complemented (in later years) by an in-depth investigation with geometrical experimentation to facilitate greater variety of formal expression. Whereas technical innovation was initially celebrated and made highly explicit (including the incorporation of structural and mechanical details, later examples of the High-tech movement (such as Foster + Partners' work with Apple) tend to carefully craft solutions where the extensive design/engineering effort becomes practically invisible.

Diametrically opposite to this style was Postmodernism,[8] where architects such as James Stirling, Mario Botta, Aldo Rossi, Terry Farrell, or Leon Krier responded to the perceived shortcomings of the Modernist movement by (re) introducing what they would consider more human-focused choice of materials, colours, spatial configurations, and construction methods in order to oppose the seemingly abstract and 'cold' appeal of glass and steel. The style embraces a Ruskinesque anti-technology sentiment that translates into a great number of choices architects considered at the time when advancing their projects.

Another counterpoint to the Modernist Movement can be seen in Deconstructivism, led by designers such as Lebbeus Woods, Peter Eisenman, Zaha Hadid, Coop Himmelb(l)au, Frank Gehry, and Morphosis.[9] Often associated with the philosophical writings of Jacques Derrida,[10] the Deconstructivists questioned the symmetrical and 'orderly' appeal of most modernist (and orthogonal) design. They introduced sharp angle-changes and dissected/fragmented planar surfaces, overall challenging the hegemony of orthogonal structural systems. In doing so, they required a major shift away from precedent-focused and standardised construction methods. Despite a dependence on existing construction methods, materials, and fabrication techniques, one aspect intrinsic to the Deconstructivism movement is to question what is technically possible in order to realise highly bespoke design solutions. In doing so, they had to embrace technology as a matter of course to master the complexity inherent to their design, both in terms of geometrical articulation, as well as forging tight relationships with engineers and fabricators to advance their daring concepts into built artefacts.

It therefore only makes sense that representatives of the Deconstructivism movement pioneered the use of digital technology for form finding and construction processes in the early 1990s. Gehry Partners, Morphosis, Coop Himmelb(l)au, and Zaha Hadid Architects all pushed new frontiers in free-form architecture by engaging with and advancing high-end software solutions, as well as reinventing

---

8 Adamson, G. and Pavitt, J. (ed.) (2011) *Postmodernism: Style and Subversion, 1970–1990*, V&A Publishing, London.

9 Johnson, P. and Wigley, M. (1988) *Deconstructivist Architecture*, Museum of Modern Art, New York.

10 Wigley, M. (1995) *The Architecture of Deconstruction, Derrida's Haunt*, MIT Press, Cambridge, MA.

the supply chain between designer and specialist contractor. Just before the turn of the millennium, design software (in particular for free-form topological modelling) started to impact contemporary practice in a way that introduced great freedom of formal expression. In turn, it helped unearth a new movement that was initially labelled 'Blob Architecture' due to the designers' ability to express their projects using double-curved/free-form geometry. Not necessarily associated with a distinct style, it was later referred to more generally as '*Digital Architecture*'[11] and was complemented with the use of parametric design techniques, leading to what some commentators tried to label 'parametricism'.[12] If this could be called a style at all, it would be the first of its kind that is strongly aligned with the (computational) tools that enabled its formal expression.

As an interesting side aspect, the introduction of more standardised and efficiency-focused Building Information Modelling processes is at times at odds with the (likely) more sophisticated modelling and project delivery practices within leading design firms. BIM might get pushed onto them via market forces that demand a more 'democratised' approach of sharing project information with clients, contractors, and other consultants. For that reason, one often finds a dichotomy within those practices, which then run 'exploratory design' and a 'design delivery (BIM)' subgroups within their Design Technology teams. Those who master this rift put resources into streamlining their technology use across conceptual design, documentation, and fabrication processes.

2.2   Becoming Strategic About Technology Choices

When asking architecture firms about their technology choices, one surprising response seems to prevail: many architecture firms arrive at their current state not via conscious decisions but rather by coincidence, being driven by ad hoc project needs rather than by a more strategic approach! They are responsive rather than proactive.

In contrast, firms excelling in this space do so via conscious decision making and by matching their design (and sometimes even 'practice') leadership with a well articulated Design Technology strategy. Instead of being driven by what technology might have to offer, they make conscious decisions on how technology gets applied to maximise its benefits for their practice. Where do they start?

The Business Case for Software Selection

A sound Design Technology strategy should go hand in hand with a business case that balances a firm's preferred way of working, its financial constraints, and the skill base among staff. Software selection needs to be strategic, even when tools are either low-cost or free. Hidden costs are associated to allowing staff to use whatever available application or plug-in they prefer: managing the choice of tools across an organisation (in particular for medium- and larger-sized firms) requires a strategic approach to maximise their benefits. Ultimately, staff need to be trained in those tools, and their use needs to be supported by the Design Technology team (or expert). If left uncoordinated, the functions across different tools may overlap substantially, which leads to a doubling-up of effort and

---

11 Campo, M. (2013) 'The Digital Turn in Architecture 1992–2012', in *AD Reader*, John Wiley & Sons, London.

12 Available at: www.parametricism.com/patrik-schumacher (Accessed: 31 October 2022).

productivity losses, if different (library) components or hardware configurations are required.

Next to the issue of 'tool anarchy' are questions about versions and the appropriate time to upgrade/update a tool. What is the trade-off between efficiency gains, the cost of the latest version, and the time/effort it takes to debug/test it in conjunction with a wider ecology of tools? One must be careful when jumping onto the latest version as soon as it is released. The new version itself may operate perfectly fine and offer productivity boost, but benefits may be jeopardised if it does not (yet) integrate well with the input/output of other applications. In particular those design practices that developed a range of custom scripts to speed up their workflow are advised to carefully check compatibility of any new software version in order to avoid sudden problems when deadlines are looming.

Design Technology experts play a pivotal role in articulating the pros and cons of different choices to practice leadership. The high cost of current CAD software requires firms to think twice before choosing any particular tool, especially if they are tied to obligatory version upgrades at frequent intervals. In addition, some more computation-intensive applications (e.g., rendering, BIM authoring, or geospatial design tools) require specific hardware specifications that put a strain on any firm's budget. It is best to develop these budgets within two- to three-year cycles, accepting a natural progression of tool choices.

One of the most prolific design firms when it comes to their strategic application of tools and technology is London-based Zaha Hadid Architects (ZHA). There, the approach to software selection and tool infrastructure is strongly tied to their bespoke design philosophy, the market they operate in (on any given project), and the overarching business drivers that govern how the firm is run.

▼ Figure 2.1

Charles Walker and Patrik Schumacher at the office.
© Dominik Holzer

ZAHA HADID ARCHITECTS

▲ Figure 2.2

Xi'an International Football Centre, render by Atchain.
© Zaha Hadid Architects

Patrik Schumacher had been the driving force behind ZHA's ability to realise highly complex projects, long before Zaha Hadid's passing in 2016. Her free-form design ambitions often preceded what was technically possible at the time. Patrik and his team(s) not only applied cutting edge technology to complement those ambitions with novel solutions, Patrik always also embedded the firm's approach within a matching design theory. As a result, ZHA have been pushing the discourse about the relationship between behaviour, process, morphology, and performance. Here, Patrik reflects on some of these approaches and explains how they impact on the way the firm integrates Design Technology on a practical level. He is joined by ZHA's director Charles Walker and by the leader of their CODE team, Shajay Bhooshan.

How do your written contributions about the contemporary discourse on architectural design (for instance, the heuristic methods you wrote for 'Parametricism') make their way into how the practice operates?

Patrik Schumacher (PS): I believe that is something that can be referred to as one of the key categories of the conceptual base of an architectural project, linked strongly with technological possibilities. That whole idea of – let us call it – Relationism comes out of tools which allow you to set up a model as a model of relations. That is an important root of parametricism; it has its own rationality, because it is all about components or spaces mutually adapting and adapting with the context. Its internal relations, as well as relations with the object itself. It relates to adaptive embedding of a project into its context but also embedding various spaces into the network of spaces. That is really, on a deep conceptional level, coming through a new set of technologies. To do that on a high level of complexity, becomes nearly impossible without the tools. The very idea comes to some extent through the tool.

On a project level, how do you ensure that the strength of the idea can be translated? In your selection of tools and tool ecologies but also the associated skills of your staff, how can you maximise the output?

PS: That is a constraint. I wrote the book *Digital Hadid*, where I showed that some of the ambitions predate the tools, but then the tools were drawn in to meet these ambitions. These tools initially came from the animation industry, science simulation, etc. But once they were in, the tools were radicalising and expanding the initial desires. They build up new desires and new concepts, so there is a dialectic. In this conversation we can emphasis the 'purpose-generation of the tool'. The tool should not only be seen relative to a pre-established purpose, but tools which come in from outside, generate new purposes, or allow us to imagine new purposes. Therefore, they become formative for the development also of styles. Like the style of Parametricism, but also subsidiary styles. I am talking about

Foldism/Blobism/Swarmism; each of these relate to new tools. The latest is a whole suite of new tools associated to Tectonism. Achieving this is challenging on a skill level; therefore we run demonstrator projects and rely on our CODE team to help us explore these. Some of this exploration then feeds into larger projects. Ultimately, I believe Tectonism is the most cost-effective of all styles.

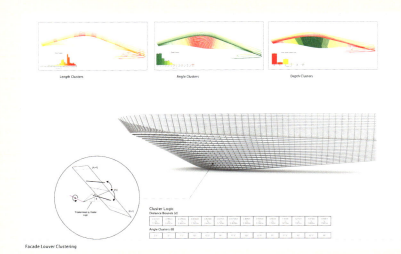

◀ Figure 2.3

Xi'an International Football Centre, façade louver clustering – cluster logic.
© Zaha Hadid Architects

In your article 'From Typology to Topology', you make the point that R&D now always has to be involved in advancing a 'cutting edge' design practice. It appears that if you want to succeed on that front, you also have to change the dialogue with your collaborators, with the engineers and others.

PS: There is a change of attitude we require. We want them to be more assertive and foreground the engineering intelligence more, rather than somehow, by whatever means necessary, realising some preconceived form. In the past, the engineers were far too subservient and keen, asking us, 'Tell us what you want, and we can make it happen'. We then tell them: 'Hey, what we want from you is structural rationality foregrounded not just: We can do this'.

▼ Figure 2.4

Beijing International Airport, interior views.
© Hufton+Crow

Beijing Airport falls under Tectonism, with its ambitious structural forms that constitute the roof. The optimised form becomes an orientation or navigation tool nearly by default. If you have a flat roof, it does not tell you where the centre of the space is. If you have a fully optimised system, the columns are tracked, and the form tells you in which direction the space is spanning, where the centre is, where the supports are, and entrances would radiate through. If you develop a sense for this, Tectonism achieves communicative capacity. The exact aesthetic outcome, I am quite relaxed about.

Realising that ZHA never works on 'typical' projects, is there still something common about the technology you apply in support of your design and delivery process?

Shajay Bhooshan (SB): Initially, the focus in a company like ZHA is always on the disruptive change that is going to happen. In that sense, we are seeking new design expressions that become feasible because of new technologies. 'Integrate' and 'disrupt' are the two major pathways; these two need to be balanced as we would not succeed to operate in a commercially viable way otherwise. For us all, technology such as Grasshopper or CATIA, things that are ready out of the box, are part of existing workflows. There is nothing new that we need to bring there. We just have to manage the dataflow and ensure the design intention transfers too. This is not terribly exciting, but it is very important. On the other side, we have stand-alone programming and being aware of the bleeding edge of research in academia and the industry; how technologies are progressing, and then developing a geometric language based on these new technologies. That is the disruptive side as far as we are concerned.

▲ Figure 2.5

Unicorn Island Master Plan.
© Zaha Hadid Architects

On a project level, how do you manage to insert that approach among your teams and the project architects at ZHA?

PS: Through project review sessions and critiques, and I hope that they read some of my texts and lectures. Many of our project architects are ex-students, so they know at least a lot of the thinking. I am pushing the CODE team into various projects; we need to network-up as we are nearly 400 staff here. We are

PRACTICE INSERT: Zaha Hadid Architects

not always fully aware of all the projects and precedence or of colleagues and co-researchers who may be relevant to new projects as inspiration. I work a small research group here at ZHA, plus four funded PhD students at the Angewandte (Academy in Vienna). There we investigate Agent-based parametric semiology. The technological aspect of that is a new level of occupancy or 'live-process' modelling. That effort connects with a group we founded to address corporate space planning. The first application arena of ABPS would be the corporate domain. This is all about social functionality simulation and enhancing social functionality via information-rich environments which empower users to orient, navigate, gather, and interact. We are talking about simulating real-world interaction processes through multi-agent models.

Which management structures are in place at ZHA to effectively apply Design Technology? How do you engage with the project directors?

PS: As an organisation, we have three front-end profit centres or 'clusters', each led by one director, and we have a CEO. We discuss in our business meetings on Monday mornings which project goes to which cluster, based on skill, experience, and so on. We also 'loan' people between clusters. Once that is set, we already know the downstream team, and then the project goes into the front design space. Later, the exact delivery methodology and workflow are developed by those [cluster] directors. Ultimately, it is at the beginning when we decide which project has which ambition. There, a 'special agenda' is set, either by the design cluster or by CODE, who – in that case – acts like a design cluster.

▼ Figure 2.6

Beyabu Honduras pilot project, digital fabrication – modular kit of parts and digital timber.
© Zaha Hadid Architects

If we talk about CODE for a moment: how many people are there – is there a 'core team? Are they a 'team for hire' that is set up separately from the project teams?

SB: The CODE group has now been operating since 2007 approximately, and we are seeing what was disruptive back then is now on the cusp of being mainstream. Our internal conversation centres around ways to transmit all the research we do to as many projects as possible. We intend to deliver disruptive change via four key channels: technologies, collaborators, internal personnel, and demonstrator projects. We devote most our efforts in at CODE on these four elements with connections to cutting-edge academia, industry, and even philosophical thinking. We try to digest all these influences and make them available to clusters one to three. There is a VR group and the Workspace group (which is about office planning).

We do what Patrik calls 'research' for about 40% of time – that is more or less the disruptive side. We do interface with project teams; sometimes we resolve façade rationalisation problems. In those cases, we are embedded in a team. It is not a consultancy in that sense. On the disruptive side, we engage in pilots and demonstrator projects, we produce 'best practice' documents, we run lectures. We contribute heavily to ZHA exhibitions, where we produce exhibition catalogues and searchable image archives. That is how knowledge is disseminated in the office. Because we are not a specialist group, we do not have a specialist budget; it is all case by case. One of the greatest things is that we are not required to make a profit in a traditional cost centre sense. At the same time, we ensure that we are not making a loss.

On what percentage of projects do you do the BIM in-house?

Charles Walker (CW): We are using a BIM tool like Revit more as an aggregator of information because it is de facto an industry standard platform. We cannot really design in Revit because it is too cumbersome for the kind of work we do. We are at the point where we have become quite fluid and able to write out own patches to carry information across platforms. Sometimes information only passes through Revit for the purpose of generating the contractually required drawings.

SB: We believe the better way to do BIM is not to simply think about it in terms of 'constant' handover, but that the toolchain itself always remains flexible. Even in the late stages we should still be able to re-initiate things in Maya and Rhino. Things need to flow, which currently does not really happen with typical BIM tools.

Is there ever a situation where your collaborating local executive architects and contractors get back to you, telling you: 'Sorry we cannot do this; we cannot document/build what you designed'.

SB: That is exactly the kind of pushback we are interested in. When they tell us they cannot do it, we ask them why. Then we try to abstract their response as a geometric constraint to make the seed itself rational rather than wait until downstream processes kick-off. At that point, we clearly ask the question whether the issue relates to a software limitation or an inherent problem with the geometry. If it is the former, it is their liability to deal with it; if it is a geometric issue, it becomes our problem. Once you abstract a problem into geometry, a wider range of mathematical tools and knowledge communities come to bear. We want to see geometry as the common glue; the language that designers understand, that engineers understand, and that computer graphics people understand.

CW: Over the past ten years of completing built projects, we have developed a network of fabricators who we know to be 'CNC-friendly'. Companies such as steel fabricators and cladding contractors. We have built our skills in terms of understanding what they require and understanding, at a greater level of detail, their techniques in making things. Casting, CNC cutting, moulds, CNC bending of metal panels, and so forth. This is one of the interesting things about digital technology: It does tend to reconnect us with fabricators or people who make things. Over the past ten to twenty years, the general contractors have de-skilled and have become more like risk managers. In a weird way we have therefore become somewhat distanced from general contractors but closer to the fabricators.

▲ Figure 2.7
Striatus 3D printed bridge, Strength Through Geometry.
© Zaha Hadid Architects

◀ Figure 2.8
Striatus 3D printed bridge, robotic fabrication and assembly in Venice.
© naaro

PRACTICE INSERT: Zaha Hadid Architects

What are the limitations of Design Technology at ZHA?

CW: If anything, I would say it is the opposite: current Design Technology has enabled us to deliver the work and to communicate the geometry. It has enabled us to prove that a project can be delivered cost-effectively via our network of collaborating fabricators. Zaha was always interested in the vanguard of architecture practice. Through Patrik's influence of introducing digital technology relatively early on, the practice has become a group of early adopters. In a way, we have been challenging industry to an extent. There is definitively a risk that things go wrong, but in a way, as architects, we are paid to take risks and manage that risk. Some practices end up dumbing down their level of ambition and try to design very similarly to what they have done before, that they know can easily be done within the constraints of the budget. Zaha would not really accept that; her ambition for the project was always at the highest level. That spirit of trying to achieve the highest level of ambition you can possibly get away with, at the same time carrying all that risk, that is what we do.

Where do you want to take ZHA in the coming years considering some of the technology that you believe is 'up and coming'?

PS: It is about redeeming and demonstrating the validity of our intuitions about Parametricism. It is about a complex, open, fluid environment that is more porous, where relationships are denser. The tools we will have at our disposition should allow us to make project-specific choices with high fidelity. Traditionally it was relatively obvious how buildings should function. It was nearly trivial, and you did not need live process modelling. On many of the larger infrastructure projects, such as those we are involved in, where people stream in from five sides, you do not know how wide certain areas or circulation spaces should be. You need to simulate bottlenecks and congestions but also determine where spaces might be underutilised. Corporations are the frontier of societal innovation; this is where progressive dynamics happen. We want to conquer the world of work.

Focus on Tool Ecologies for Exploratory Design

When choosing software within a Design Technology context, it soon becomes apparent that each application cannot solely be judged on its own merit. Architecture firms do not apply their software solutions in isolation; instead they seek for connectivity among a series of tools that support their desired workflow. Interoperability across multiple tools and the setup of tool ecologies are primary concerns when developing a Design Technology strategy. Not only do these investigations consider the technical aspect of linking information from different sources, but they also consider the resulting changes to the workflow between architects and their collaborators. For example, when combining parametric design setups with analysis tools, architects are now able to test their designs in close to real time against any types of performance criteria.

The key association suggested here in reference to the increasing connectivity of our design and analysis tools is 'convergence'.[13] Convergence in the field has taken place as a crossover not only from geometric modelling to performance simulation and analysis tools but also (and more recently) from early exploratory design towards object-oriented design documentation and delivery tools.

Another key contributing factor to the increased digital convergence in the design studio is the change to the tool infrastructure available to architects and their collaborators. Design firms can check for trends and interrogate their early concept models across different domains, be it structural behaviour, environmental sustainability, cost, constructability, ease of fabrication, and more. For this to occur, Design Technology specialists in those firms are typically concerned with overcoming issues of tool interoperability and with the most logical pathway of connecting different applications to suit a project team's workflow.

These opportunities are not simply affecting tool choices, but they have a fundamental impact on process, communication, and design authorship. Digitally advanced design firms often embrace opportunities for co-rationalisation between architects and engineers instead of a sequential process, where feedback loops between different stakeholders can take days (or sometimes even weeks) to accomplish. Optioneering in close to real time as a process for collaboration becomes a possibility when designers advance their ideas in early-stage design.

Major progress has been achieved in the integration between parametric modelling and building performance optimisation in the period 2005–2015. As the use of associative modelling and performance analysis became mainstream in the architectural design studio, architects started connecting their associative models with an ever growing number of plug-ins for building performance evaluation.

In reflection on the progress within this period, several key developments stand out:

- The erosion of the boundaries between tools for architectural design and engineering analysis. There is an increasing notion that these tools are being applied by either group.
- Greater interoperability between geometric modelling for design morphology and performance simulation/analysis functions with less dependence on export to third-party tools for calculations/appropriations of data.
- Increased user-friendliness of interfaces that appeal to a more visually driven design approach by architects. Visual scripting combined with graphic user

---

13 Deutsch, R. (2017) *Convergence: The Redesign of Design*, AD Smart05, John Wiley & Sons Ltd., Hoboken, NJ.

interfaces and a 3D model environment appeals to architects more than text-based data entry. Better interpretation of analysis results as colour-coded flow charts, surface renders, or plotted graphs. These explicit display options allow non-specialists to interpret results and understand underlying performance trends more intuitively than mere numeric output.

- Increased availability and access to tools that perform – in basic terms – the kind of analysis that architects would engage in. Whereas in the past many analysis functions were deeply embedded in often high-price specialist engineering software, these functions can now be called via free plug-ins that connect straight to the tool infrastructure available to students.
- Opportunities to maintain associations across parametric modulation and building performance analysis. This has resulted in a fluid transfer of data related to a design's morphology and resulting changes to its physical building performance.
- In general, and related to the preceding points, an increased understanding by architectural students about the (combined) impact of various design performance feedback on the morphological development of their design. This results in more conscious decision making, enhancing a student's ability to argue convincingly why certain design solutions had been chosen over others.
- A better understanding about the delineations of what architects should know about building performance in contrast to what information they should query from their engineering counterparts.

2.3 Matching Studio Culture With Technology Support

There is no single approach for architecture firms to determine whether, when, and how to apply technology to support their design. Choices depend on a great variety of factors, starting from the size of a practice, the type of projects it delivers, the market it operates in, the capabilities of its collaborators, and, last but not least, the specific design approach taken by those running the firm.

How does a design firm select the right tools to support their way of working? What tools and infrastructure should be in place to allow a practice to operate in the best possible way? Who is most suited to make decisions about Design Technology, and how is the implementation of Design Technology managed on an organisational level?

Starting With Culture and Business Drivers, Not With Technology!

Considerations of a firm's cultural particularities must be made at the outset of any conversation that relates its design approach to a matching tool ecology. The way technology is applied and deciding who becomes responsible to look after its proliferation either are influenced directly by the philosophy of its founding member(s) or relates to management decisions that have been made along the way. Within the competitive global market we experience today, how a firm positions itself stands in direct relation to the technology they apply in order to become/remain distinctive and successful.

The conversation about a design firm's studio culture and its associated relation to technology and management approaches is not new. In 1987, Weldon Coxe and his co-authors reflected on their consulting experience in practice when proposing the Superpositioning Model.[14] There, they distinguished three main types of architecture and engineering firms, namely those predominantly focusing on ideas, on service, and on delivery. It is important for firms to understand where their emphasis lies and how they want to position themselves in the market to be successful. Whereas ideas-oriented firms take risks to innovate, experiment, and explore new and unique paths for each project, service-oriented firms depend strongly on the expertise and long-lasting commitment of their employees to push the boundaries of what is possible, backed up by a proven track record of previously successful approaches. Delivery-oriented firms aim at specialising in a building sector where issues from project to project are highly repetitive and budgetary constraints are of the highest importance.

Coxe and his co-authors demonstrate that not one singular type but different types of support are needed to make a firm successful in their specific market. This has strong implications on the design ideology, staff recruitment, and knowledge exchange between designers, consultants, and contractors as well as the technical and organisational support.

With over thirty years after its first publication, many aspects of the Superpositioning Model still stack up. Yet the architecture profession has also undergone dramatic change over this period. Communication among project participants has intensified, the speed of project delivery has gone up significantly, and rigid office structures have become more flexible to respond to a fast and volatile global market. We have also seen the emergence of large, globally operating architecture firms with several satellite offices. It may simply be unrealistic to expect their entire operation to follow one unified approach. They have to embrace local differences, and they are likely to combine delivery/service/ideas-focused designers under one roof.

Setting Boundaries

Anyone dealing with technology in the context of architectural design soon realises that the potential to introduce new digital workflows and associated tools is unlimited. This realisation comes with a warning: without a clear strategy, embracing technology in support of design can become a bottomless pit. When developing a firm's DT strategy, it is therefore pivotal to set clear boundaries on how far technology should play a role in the way the practice is set up. Is Design Technology simply a means to an end? Is it a factor to drive innovation through a practice? Can it help to distinguish the firm from its competition via a highly bespoke approach? What budget should the practice spend on Design Technology, and what exactly should they spend it on?

As a simple starting point, one could count the different tools used in the practice at any given day (you might be surprised how many tools are in use already). What are they for? Are any of those similar to others and potentially double up? Should some of them be phased out? Are any tools missing?

These are basic questions that at best will assist the firm to consolidate their efforts and introduce a more conscious use of technology across the practice. Yet more relevant questions remain. Should one really invest in a new VR goggle, knowing perfectly well that next year's model will have double the resolution? What are the productivity gains of one tool/hardware vs. another, in particular when considering that continuous change is inherent to any tool selection? A Design Technology strategy needs to balance these questions and factor in

---

14 Coxe, W., et al. (1987) *Success Strategies for Design Professionals: SuperPositioning for Architecture & Engineering Firms*, McGraw-Hill, New York.

time spent on testing, debugging, staff training, and alignment with existing tool ecologies.

What time should be spent on tool development and customisation? Any architecture firm embracing Design Technology will hit a point where they need to ask themselves: 'With our core-business deeply rooted in design, how deep do we want to delve into software development?' Ultimately design remains the breadwinner, and the development of digital applications cannot always be costed against projects. How relevant are the new tools that get developed compared to the effort it takes to do so? Every practice will have a different sweet spot in responding to this question. It is therefore pivotal for upper management to set clear targets and boundaries to the use of technology that are in sync with both their business model as well as their design philosophy.

Dealing With Resistance

Technology is not equally embraced by everyone. Designers in particular are trained to rely on their instincts and their creative side to advance their projects. The sketch that flows immediately from the hand, the curious mind that translates thought into some lines on a napkin – these are the weapons of choice for many. Whatever comes next can be seen as diminishing the initial concept or, even worse, killing off creativity. For many, the thought of designing by 'spreadsheet' or relying on computer software to advance ideas would be diametrically opposed to that creative process.[15] In other words, and relating back to Ruskin's technoscepticism, Design Technology can be met with substantial resistance by those who see their creative side threatened by it or by those who simply reject it due to misconceptions and anxieties about handing control over design decisions to a machine.

These anxieties should not easily be dismissed by those responsible for Design Technology in a practice setting. The anxieties can result in tangible concerns and frustrations by staff members who feel alienated by technology instead of being supported by it. If these sentiments persist, it can give those who promote technological advance a bad name, as they encounter resistance in their efforts to propagate Design Technology across the practice. Even worse, if leadership is not fully on board with the technology solutions offered by their experts, it can create a rift in the practice that sidelines Design Technology and minimises its potential.

To overcome resistance, the best way forward is to search for maximum alignment between the desired workflow of key individuals and the digital tools that are available. This calls for technologists to become very familiar with the workflow of different design leaders within an architecture firm and to then introduce them to novel technology within the constraints of their comfort zone. Senior design staff within practice cannot be expected to be aware of or even to have tested the latest and greatest digitally supported tools or processes on the market. It is therefore the task of the Design Technology team to bring those tools/processes to their attention and show them how they could interact with their current workflow.

One practice that excelled their engagement in this space is NYC-based Diller Scofidio + Renfo. Their oeuvre (as illustrated by a great range of built work in recent years, across a number of different continents) exemplifies mastery in integrating the functional, aesthetic, material, and performance aspects of their design.

---

15 Lawson, B. (2002) 'CAD and Creativity: Does the Computer Really Help?', *Leonardo*, 35 (3), pp. 327–331.

CHAPTER 2 Positioning Technology Within Design Practice

57

▼ Figures 2.9
The Broad, 3D sections.
Courtesy of Diller Scofidio + Renfo

DILLER SCOFIDIO + RENFO

PRACTICE INSERT: Diller Scofidio + Renfo

Diller Scofidio + Renfo frequently challenge existing design conventions by exploring novel and highly innovative solutions. The arts background of the studio principals is thereby never at odds with technological advance, and instead they embrace it to strengthen their unique approach to the design and delivery of their projects. As a true maestro in the use of the image editing software Photoshop, Ric Scofidio explains how digital tools are not just limited to sophisticated 3D modelling but often relate back to a designer's craft. At the same time, technology offers a way to explore the impossible, or, as Ric calls it (quoting Leonard Cohen), 'The cracks are how the light gets in'. Here he is joined by former DS+R Computational Design architect Matthew Ostrow, whose input was pivotal on some of the studio's recent projects.

What role does Design Technology play at Diller Scofidio + Renfro? How do you implement it to support your distinctive design approach?

Matthew Ostrow (MO): When I joined DS+R, the office had twenty-five people, and we did not do any 3D modelling. Working via 2D CAD and hand-drawing was the norm. Over the past few years, meetings in our office have graduated from having no screens (there were models and drawings instead) to – at times – an extreme opposite where we are spinning digital models around and looking at things in real time, while making adjustments on the fly.

 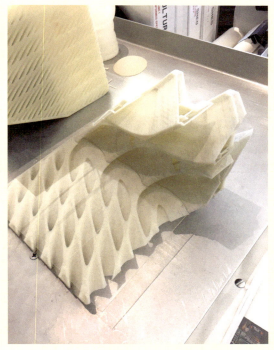

▲ Figure 2.10

The Broad, working models and built façade/roof veil.
© Dominik Holzer

PRACTICE INSERT: Diller Scofidio + Renfo

▲ Figure 2.10
(Continued)

The models we use are made in a way that allows us to live-edit almost everything. A partner or principal can 'feel-out' and get inside the model and look at angles and so forth. If we are designing a concert hall, you can sit in different seats, which is especially helpful if you are dealing with a moving building like The Shed. The Shed is very complicated given the fact that you are moving a building over a building. There was a lot of design influence that came from being able to explore digitally in 3D, not just through drawings or physical models. We were able to incorporate more movement into the design of The Shed thanks to the use of 3D software. However, we also make projects that are more distinctly on the analogue side.

Which management structures do you have in place to apply Design Technology at DS+R?

MO: We have an in-house IT manager who is versed enough in our software to keep us all pretty tight. That being said, he does not set up the way we use Revit. That is managed in-house as well, but we do not have a formal BIM Manager. We do have a Revit usergroup that meets a couple of times a month to check in on how people are doing with their projects and to ensure that everybody understands what's new in the software. Oversight is also provided via three colleagues who have expertise in BIM. As for CATIA, I am probably the only person in the studio who uses it on projects every day, and the only person generating geometry with it right now. We currently do not have a project in design that is CATIA based – our projects typically do not start that way.

Are there sometimes any cultural clashes between the design approach and technology/technologists at DS+R?

Ricardo Scofidio (RS): I do think it is important to know the tools that are at your disposal. I find that when I am on the computer, I tend to be more rule observant than when I am drawing by hand. That manual process pulls me into areas that I am stupidly going into. It is a process that is open and should remain open.

▲ Figures 2.11

Example of Photoshop use by Ric Scofidio, blur building rendering.
Courtesy of Diller Scofidio + Renfro

My first real experience using digital design tools was Photoshop, which was a lame tool in its early versions but became quite an incredible tool as it evolved. But if you ask somebody else to do something in Photoshop for you, you go crazy. Because everybody uses it differently – everybody uses it their own way. The great thing about Photoshop is that you can get to an answer in the most incredible ways. I am a MAC guy; I do not work PCs. I am sure that everybody is approaching these things in a different way. That difference is what is going to crack it open and produce something you did not expect.

How does the process work at DS+R? On a typical project, how does it get initiated? Do you work with napkin sketches?

RS: There is no particular way to approach a project. At Cooper Union, the one thing I noticed was that, when the school was finally able to access computers and start using them, they approached them totally differently because their background was in sketching, drawing, and model making. They approached them differently than someone would who did not have that background. Someone who may only have computer skills tends to get locked into them. I therefore believe it is important, and I know this is what happens in our studio, that people sketch, people draw, and people make models. There is a whole plethora of stuff that we do to get to where we want to be.

How do the Design Technology experts at DS+R operate, and how do they interact with the project teams?

MO: DS+R is not an expert-based studio, although there are people who collaborate with several project teams at once because they have a certain expertise. They are generally on the younger side, working on gaining experience in the office and finding out where they fit. They contribute in different ways and often have a skill that is valuable in a few different situations.

◀ Figure 2.12

Matthew Ostrow and Ric Scofidio in conversation.
© Dominik Holzer

Do these staff have an aspiration to become project architects, or do they want to become Rhino/Revit/CATIA experts? Your example shows that they can be both.

MO: I would rather teach somebody the innards of a machine than the software. But we do not strictly look for experts in a specific software. Of course, you need to hire a Revit expert because there is such an enormous effort that needs to be put into certain projects, but we would generally hire somebody who will be a valuable well rounded person who also brings that skill to the table. When I was hired, Liz said: 'I only hire misfits, I hire only the weird ones, I only hire people who do not fit in anywhere else.'

At DS+R, is it technology just a means to an end, is it a major driver of innovation and creativity, or somewhere in between?

RS: You cannot have design without technology! Even dating back to caveman times, the moment you introduce design, you are into technology. I feel strongly (and I do not know why I developed this as a point of view) that technology should not be forefronted. It is all about design. Technology is there to use as a tool to achieve the design you want. It is such an obvious known quality. From early discussions on projects, I do not want people to focus on how do they do that . . . or get sucked into . . . what is the technology to do this or that. I also think that the value of technology varies depending on what your need is. Being able to achieve things and get a real-time result to visualise ideas more rapidly is really what the visual world brings to us. We quite often do things that seem impossible, that cannot be done. We do not see any technology as a closed end or something that has a finite possibility. It is like this old Leonard Cohen song: 'The cracks are how the light gets in'. The point is that if you run into something that seems impossible to do, you can use technology to find an answer. You might open up an entire new area of investigation you can push.

How would you describe the ecology of tools you apply?

MO: Much of the benefit that technology gives us these days derives from being able to visualise our ideas. DS+R's use of Design Technology started with laid-out or drafted-out axonometries and perspectives where Ric filled in imagery. Ric has a way of working in Photoshop that is so beautiful; it is a collage-based approach. He'll paint in things, and yet he has an amazing clarity. I have seen Ric come in on day two of a competition and have a full concept that he articulates through words but also through a beautiful Photoshop picture. At that point it is not strictly architecture; it is a concept. In many instances, you share a 'feel-book' with clients that includes images of what the project is supposed to feel like. They are usually very beautiful and composed with a slight sense of humour.

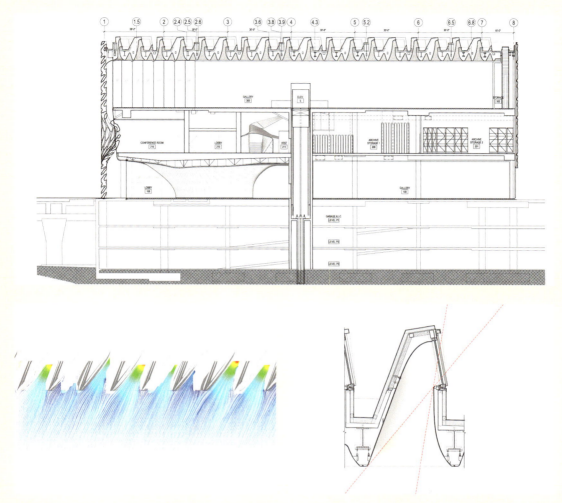

▲ Figure 2.13

The Broad, façade section, daylighting model for even daylight distribution, and detail section of skylight.
Courtesy of Diller Scofidio + Renfro

Other than Photoshop, half the staff in the studio use 3DsMax. We do our own animations in-house and outsource some camera-path scenario renderings. Most of our independent art projects require visual art and interactive aspects.

Are you using any parametric software?

MO: We frequently use Grasshopper in the office, as we experiment with form a lot. During concept design, its use is based on efficiency gains. In later phases, we use it on projects that get complicated from a geometric perspective. We have a number of highly proficient Grasshopper users in the office, but they may also switch over to Revit based on the projects they work on. The best way to explain is as follows: the type of project and where in the world we are building it determine which technology and software we use to derive the parts and pieces being brought to the job.

On some projects we rely heavily on the use of CATIA. One such example is The Shed. In a way, The Shed is almost three buildings in one. The structure housing all the kinetic components was controlled in CATIA. It was a necessity to have heavy engineering done on basic information: union-to-node, centre of gravity, and control-centre of gravity of every structural member. As the architect, when you have to interact on an engineering level or a façade level, that aspect becomes dependent on your precision regarding the geometric and manufacturing information that gets distributed.

Once the CATIA file gets heavy, we save it to Revit. We manage the information flow between CATIA and Revit via a translation tool. As part of our export process from CATIA, we only bring things into Revit that are necessary. For the documentation that comes out of Revit, we developed a process where we take the CATIA file, extract the information, and then just clean it up in AutoCAD. The final drawing set has a lot to do with these three software applications.

◀ Figure 2.14

The Shed, close-up of custom structural steel elements of retractable façade.
© Dominik Holzer

As for more 'standard' documentation aspects, we have become very proficient in BIM, now that many clients require Revit-level models as a deliverable. We have our in-house Revit team who do 3D coordination and documentation on projects. About a third of the people in our studio are somewhere between advanced and serious users of Revit. Overall, a third of our staff is very fluent in both Rhino and Revit.

Are you comparing notes with your offices, and how do you collaborate with them when it comes to advancing and applying Design Technology?

MO: As in all offices, staff numbers fluctuate, and DS+R currently employs just over a hundred people. The vast majority are located in New York, but we also have a few people in London and in Australia. Design work happens nearly exclusively at our New York office, and hence the key drive for Design Technology happens here.

What are the limitations of Design Technology use at DS+R?

MO: To be frank, for a while we wondered: "Do we invest in Design Technology tools? How heavily should the office invest in hardware?" It was not a software problem. Rather, there was a tipping point sometime in 2012–2014 when we had to decide how much to invest in hardware. Our projects were getting more complex. If you are designing a project in Hudson Yards or doing work on the High Line, it is at such a massive scale. The office decided to really invest in hardware at that moment.

From a cultural perspective: Are there instances where Technology gets in the way?

MO: When I started designing about ten years ago, there was a lot of value and time – you used to spend hours and hours (if not days) on a file – put into producing good Photoshop images. This is now happening less frequently. There is still a strong belief in this process among our leadership, but more and more we are starting to generate graphics from software. The other day, I opened an older Photoshop file we were working on for a press release. I realised how much you really pay attention to every detail in an image. That is a situation when technology may have gotten in the way a little, because today you can just generate a rendering from a program and include it in a competition to illustrate the ideal sunset. But in reality, it does not quite have the same feel and texture as the images that had been worked on for hours back then.

What would you like to be doing right now, that you currently cannot yet achieve?

RS: I am strangely very happy where I am and with what we are doing. When faxes were introduced, people were very excited. And then email arrived, and we started to become overwhelmed by emails. Liz is currently getting about 300 emails a day; she cannot deal with it. Whatever that future is, I want it to be something that will not overwhelm me. Something I can control and push back on when I have to rather than just being a sponge for it.

▶ Figure 2.15

The Shed, retractable façade seen from the outside.
© Dominik Holzer

PRACTICE INSERT: Diller Scofidio + Renfo

2.4 Addressing Design Technology on an Organisational Level

Looking at Design Technology in the context of organisational hierarchies or simply the way it integrates with other management aspects of a design firm, a few questions come to mind. What structures and management frameworks should practices have in place to roll out Design Technology across their organisation? How can the efforts of individuals or of dedicated Design Technology groups be coordinated in the most effective way? How do those looking after Design Technology interact with other design-, research-, and management-related groups within a firm? How do these individuals or teams need to be supported to maximise their input, and what output should be expected from them?

These questions immediately raise concerns about a 'best-fit' with the core activities undertaken in design firms. Knowledge management across projects and the dedication of 'overhead' resources to support the design process have never been the particular strength of the architectural profession. Brian Lawson,[16] architecture theorist and long-standing commentator on architectural practice, argues that the design team has become such an obvious organisational structure that most architecture offices put nearly all their human resources into these teams. More often than not, innovation and experimentation occur on a project level. Yet tight budgets and frequent submission deadlines make it very hard for staff to step back, consolidate learnings, and reflect on how that knowledge can inform office-wide procedures or add to body of work undertaken by others.

How can firms capitalise on the existing technology skills within their practice and work towards a more targeted way of supporting their teams? Design Technology has been around in architecture firms for decades, and, in most instances, the formation of a Design Technology team is preceded by prior (yet often uncoordinated) efforts in this space. Formalising their efforts into a dedicated team or fostering a group of 'Super-users'[17] aims to synergise their input and provide an umbrella for related activities.

2.5 Setting Up and Positioning Design Technology Within the Office Structure

The turning point for positioning Design Technology successfully within a practice occurs when its leadership becomes strategic about it from a business perspective. They need to realise how to connect core business activities with 'best-fit' technology solutions and support. Once they do, they then assign dedicated resources to address Design Technology across the firm in a managed and sustained way.

Initial questions may include: who will look after Design Technology, both in terms of high-level decision making, as well as in terms of on-the-floor support? What will this effort include, and how do Design Technology activities within the practice relate to one another? What budget needs to be set aside for Design Technology matters? How many people should be involved in this effort, and how can their roles be managed either next to or apart from their project-related duties? What is the potential of DT team members to contribute to the research

---

16 Lawson, B. (1997) *How Designers Think – The Design Process Demystified*, Architectural Press, Hudson, NY.
17 Randy Deutsch describes this 'new breed' of design professionals in his 2019 book: *Super Users* (Routledge).

and development efforts within the practice? How does the Design Technology team (or their subgroups) operate from a budgetary perspective? To what extent are their activities seen as an overhead or a project-related cost? How will the DT team interact with the IT team?

Feedback provided from the leading practices who took part in the research for this publication points toward multiple possible ways in which DT activities are organised within firms. It often depends on the size of the firm and their leadership structure. It also depends on the way upper management wants to be involved and informed about DT-related activities and how the typical office 'chain of command' interfaces with technological progress and delivery support. On one end of the spectrum, Design Technology resources get costed against individual projects only; on the other end, large DT teams operate as over-head and are horizontally integrated across the organisation. In many instances, architecture firms will operate between those two extremes. Three options are described reflecting scenarios that frequently occurred within the leading prac-tices who took part in the interviews for this book:

- The technology-enabled Design Architect (Coop Himmelb(l)au/DS+R/SO-IL/LASSA).
- The In-house Consultancy (H&deM/Heatherwick Studio/BIG/Morphosis/ZHA/Foster + Partners/Morphosis).
- The Global Specialist Network (Woods Bagot/Hassell/Gensler/SOM/) among others.

If we look at these three in more detail, a number of characteristics that stand out for why any particular approach gets taken.

The Technology-enabled Design Architect

The interviews revealed a common trend among small and medium-scale firms: They all tried to avoid separating their technology experts from their design experts. In other words, at firms like Coop Himmelb(l)au, Diller Scofidio + Renfo, SO-IL and LASSA, a select number of project architects not only look after the design side of things, but they also cover the technology aspect. Given the not-too-large office size, there exists a lot of cross-fertilisation and sharing of knowledge from one project to another. Office leadership trusts their staff to directly share their experience and lessons learned for Design Technology roll-out across projects. This only becomes a problem if key staff leave the firm.

The technology-enabled Design Architect may at times work with addi-tional technology support, but overall design skills are very closely tied to tech-nology savviness, often with direct contact of the designer with the fabricators and other supply-chain members. This works predominantly for technology sup-porting early design exploration but also links between design and fabrication. The 'middle part', namely BIM skills for documentation, are frequently exempt from this setup.

The In-house Specialist Group(s)

As practices grow beyond a certain point, one potential pathway in managing expert input is to start forming specialist groups (or at least appoint dedicated experts) devoted to assisting the rest of the practice with dedicated solutions.

The activities carried out by these groups span from hands-on practical support for model making all the way to highly sophisticated scripting and interfaces to academia via research activities.

Formed in 1997, Foster + Partners' Specialist Modelling Group[18] (SMG) is an early example of an in-house specialist team, such is Arup's Advanced Geometry Unit[19] (founded in 2000) and Frank Gehry's Gehry Technologies[20] division that was formed in 2002. Over the years, these groups have provided their practices invaluable input on the feasibility and buildability of complex geometrical solutions, combining computer, structural, material science and in-depth knowledge of applied geometry. Members of specialist groups (also referred to as 'computational designers') helped to interpret free-form design and rationalise it using panelisation techniques (to avoid double curvature and introduce repeatability) or other types of geometry subdivisions that can easily and cost-effectively be manufactured and installed (such as ruled-surfaces). Geometry rationalisation did not remain the sole activity of computational designers. It included the use of evolutionary techniques for finding design solutions via automated search algorithms.

With the progressing availability of performance analysis tools in the mid-2000s, the specialist teams became more and more involved in testing early-stage structural and environmental factors such as shading coefficients, solar (heat) gain, glare, and others. Many specialist groups started engaging directly with manufacturers and building fabrication and cost constraints into the scripts they developed.

Until the late 2000s, specialist groups often required designers to have C#, C++, or other programming skills. They frequently had to develop their own bespoke interfaces to link data from one tool to another. With the advent of the parametric Rhino/Grasshopper infrastructure, a lot of functions became available as plug-ins (some paid, some for free), which got shared among power users and fed into food4Rhino, the online plug-in community service by Rhino's developer McNeel. In that sense, many targeted functions that specialist groups would seek to implement have now become available to the wider public, allowing users with no or simple Python scripting abilities to enrich their tool palette.

Even the world's most innovative and technologically advanced firms do not seem to escape the need for BIM output, particularly in those cases where the client or the main contractor is requesting it. For this reason, architecture firms around the world have formed dedicated BIM groups to assist in setting out their BIM delivery approach in an efficient and cost-effective way. Due to their output focus and to avoid being confronted with constant major design changes, these groups sometimes act in isolation from the 'up-front designers'. Nevertheless, there are attempts to interface between design exploration and BIM-related workflows. Parametric data manipulation using applications such as ADSK's Dynamo or Rhino Inside assist with this effort.

When specialist groups (or individuals) provide Design Technology assistance within a design firm, questions emerge as to how their input gets coordinated and managed. Feedback from the practices interviewed for this book points towards multiple possible scenarios. These scenarios are closely tied to the question of how far Design Technology support is costed against individual projects or classified as overhead. In some cases, a Design Technology member acts

---

18 Available at: https://archive.bridgesmathart.org/2006/bridges2006-9.pdf (Accessed: 31 October 2022).
19 Available at: https://aefirms.wordpress.com/2011/01/27/arup-advanced-geometry-unit/ (Accessed: 31 October 2022).
20 Available at: www.crunchbase.com/organization/gehry-technologies (Accessed: 31 October 2022).

as 'ambassador' to the project team and gets integrated into their team structure (Heatherwick Studio). In other cases, members of the Design Technology team are 'on call' to aid whenever the design team members require additional input, intermittently across various project stages (Foster + Partners, Herzog & de Meuron). As a matter of course, the integration of Design Technology support on an organisational level is tied to the way a practice is managed. For larger firms working internationally, two scenarios are most common: a centralised approach where various support groups are concentrated in one main office (where the firm's leadership is located) or a distributed approach where various specialist groups operate in different geographic locations whilst being highly networked across one another.

With the former scenario, most decisions happen top-down in the 'headquarters' office, with the satellite (often site) offices receiving dedicated support from them (individual Design Technology staff members from the HQ are assigned to work and co-locate with them temporarily). A key designer in the HQ aims to keep design decisions and associated technology support as close to them as possible. Experimentation, testing, even the elaboration of bespoke manufacturing solutions occur at the headquarters. When projects in local offices require this specialist support, they lodge an application for the specialist team to get involved (BIG/Foster + Partners).

The Global Specialist Network

For more commercially oriented firms with a distributed leadership structure across ten, twenty, or more offices in different continents, it is not uncommon to share resources across their office network (globally). There may be 'hot-spots' where specialist groups focus one bespoke aspect of Design Technology. At the same time, the continuous exchange of staff, sophisticated networking and communication tools, plus an in-house online knowledge platform, assist in the dissemination of Design Technology–related information and support. Many of the larger offices have their own Design Technology team, and activities are coordinated with colleagues in the 'hotspots'/regional HQs. Globally operating, architecture and engineering firms such as Gensler, KPMJ, Arup, Grimshaw, Woods-Bagot, or HASSELL (just to name a few) subscribe to this model.

Design Technology is likely seen as one of the core business streams, with a dedicated global Design Technology Lead, reporting directly to the firm's leadership team (or being part of it). Individual offices have their local Design Technology leaders in different geographic locations who look after visualisation, computational design (parametric modelling/performance optimisation/links to fabrication), and BIM efforts. The local approach to Design Technology always remains closely tied to the 'global' effort within the distributed leadership structure. The global Design Technology Lead coordinates with all the local leaders and ensures that knowledge is disseminated across the entire practice. This approach requires a highly disciplined way of working with substantial emphasis put on coordination and cross-fertilisation of technology-related skills across teams. Within this model, specialists frequently visit different offices to ensure that everyone is informed about what the firm considers its global best-practice. If novel tools and processes need to be introduced, the Design Technology lead may appoint a specialist to 'flip' individual offices by embedding them within an office for an extended period, in order to provide dedicated training to staff.

Naturally, within these globally distributed firms, there exist local differences in how technology can be applied, related to market idiosyncrasies, local regulations, different salary/fee structures, etc. The Design Technology leadership needs to be aware of these to devise a strategy that guarantees efficiency gains due to a standardised approach, while still allowing for those local differences to occur. If a firm has a distinctive design approach, their support infrastructure needs to be built around the inherent processes associated to it. One such example can be seen at Heatherwick Studio, where three groups (Ge-CoDe, Immersive Media, and BIM) represent the backbone of Design Technology support. Jointly they complement Heatherwick Studio's distinct approach that is often based on physical artefacts, materiality, and prototyping. The teams assist staff in moving fluidly across physical model prototypes, digital sketches, immersive 3D worlds, all the way to documentation and fabrication of detailed componentry.

▶ Figure 2.16
The Vessel, Hudson Yards.
© Dominik Holzer

HEATHERWICK STUDIO

Thomas Heatherwick probably sits closer to product design than to architecture (or urban design). Yet his studio is responsible for some of the most recognisable architectural projects around the globe in recent years. Seemingly freed from typical architectural conventions, the Studio stays true to its origins in product design, as physical and virtual prototyping go hand in hand with material research, geometry optimisation, and close collaboration with fabricators. As Heatherwick Studio's Head of Geometry & Computational Design, Pablo Zamorano reflects on their bespoke Design Technology approach.

What role does Design Technology play at Heatherwick?

Pablo Zamorano (PZ): The main role of Digital Design at Heatherwick studio is to enable ideas to be explored, tested, documented, and realised. At Heatherwick Studio, our approach to achieving extraordinary results unfolds from making and prototyping design solutions; this includes crafting the design processes both physically and digitally. The studio has always maintained an experimental approach in the way we use tools, materials, and processes. We push the limits of how certain materials can be used, and we use technology to help us explore how certain geometry can be achieved. We continuously question the digital tools and techniques we apply in design and manufacturing.

Allowing for flexibility is key for us. The way we design, we try not to focus on one specific result but to craft processes that allow for multiple results to unfold. This means that one designer will easily produce ten options per day; this is where computing can be very helpful. Although Thomas is a maker at heart, he embraces the benefits that technology can bring which allow us to do things with some materials that would not otherwise be feasible.

As a practice, we maintain links with institutions that explore emergent technologies and digital craft. We have collaborated with IAAC in Barcelona, the Architectural Association (AA) and the Bartlett in London, among others. We embrace technology and understand its value but never only for the sake of technology; what we care about are ideas and how technology can enable us to realise them. Without the use of technology, there would be no other way to realise many of our designs.

◀ Figure 2.17

Pablo Zamorano in the London Studio.
© Dominik Holzer

▲ Figure 2.18

IAAC Collaboration Advanced Craft, IAAC Workshop, student work.
© Heatherwick Studio

How does this unfold on a practical level? Thomas's background is in product design rather than architecture. Does this change the way design unfolds within the practice?

Thomas comes from a 'designer/maker' background, and physical interaction with prototypes and models is a key way in which we test and review design ideas. Our workshop plays a key role in this process. At the same time, Thomas has always been interested in digital technology to advance and realise his vision. As a consequence, we constantly explore new digital processes that enhance the way in which we design and make, but never losing the craft or the human connection of being makers. This is how we end up crafting processes in addition to crafting objects or models.

How is Design Technology integrated at Heatherwick on an organisational level?

PZ: Digital Design is composed of three main branches, Geometry and Computational Design (Ge-CoDe), Immersive Media and BIM. Ge-CoDe and BIM have their own heads of departments, and Immersive Media works as a cluster under The head of Ge-CoDe. The Ge-Code team is composed of five computational designers, one Computational Design Intern, and ten Geometry Leads (designers), the BIM team consists of our Head of BIM, one BIM Manager, two BIM Coordinators, and two BIM Technicians, and we have one Immersive Media specialist. Ge-CoDe staff split their billed time between Projects and Applied Research.

The main tools we use are Rhino and Grasshopper, although some of the Ge-CoDe team members work with other tools such as Python, C#, etc. Their interests and knowledge also vary from advanced fabrication, environmental analysis, and data visualisation to Machine Learning and AI. The BIM and Immersive Media teams split their time mainly between assisting on the delivery of projects and capturing and sharing knowledge.

Based on what you said earlier, I would imagine you also have to employ staff with an in-depth understanding of fabrication.

PZ: Although fabrication knowledge is not a prerequisite for new joiners, it is an important aspect of what Ge-CoDe does. Especially more senior members have experience working directly with fabricators. Prototyping at one to one is also key for us, and we are lucky to have a dedicated making team in the workshop that help us in prototyping. We work in a constant loop between physical and digital crafting. This does not mean that everybody in the studio knows how to control a piece of fabrication equipment. But we try to have sufficient understanding to have informed conversations, build up good relationships with people/fabricators who can do that.

We also explore ideas that we have not yet been able to realise due to lack of technology, and we investigate new and advanced manufacturing methods we can use now to make these ideas become real. An example of this is our collaboration with the Master in Robotics and Advanced Construction where we have been exploring the use of robotics to realise our Cloud Bridge Project. Scale is also a key thing we consider when reviewing design, and the screen often takes you away from the understanding of scale. We are now using Mixed Reality to interact with the design digitally while overlapping the experience with the physical world. We also use these tools for production in the workshop so the boundaries between digital and physical are now much blurrier than they used to be.

◀ Figure 2.19

Online Hackathon collaboration, Thornton Tomasseti.
© Heatherwick Studio

Which management structures do you have in place to effectively apply Design Technology at Heatherwick Studio?

PZ: The studio is organised in domains. Digital Design is part of the projects domain. Each project in our studio gets developed by a dedicated team, consisting of a project lead and team including one Geometry Lead, stemming from the Ge-CoDe group. Two of our Computational Designers work across projects, and our Computational Design intern focuses primarily on research. BIM coordinators work across multiple projects, enabling the teams on the delivery through BIM. Immersive Media assist (on a booking basis) with the use of game engines as design tools and the delivery of animations and visuals on projects. The making team consists of about ten staff in our workshop. The workshop has many tools from a traditional making shop, plus a robust set of digital prototyping tools including 3D printers, laser cutters, and a CNC machine.

Are there sometimes cultural clashes between the design approach and Technology/Technologists at Heatherwick Studio?

PZ: We are lucky that our Geometry Leads and our Immersive Media specialist are designers and are actively engaged in projects. This has helped through the years to spread the knowledge and exposure of the benefits of technology in our process. Some of the team members are now project leaders, and that has also helped to champion the use of technology through projects. There are still times, however, where some teams may think that a problem may be solved quicker by hand and avoid the use of computation; however, these cases are now rare. For BIM coordinators, we try to ensure that they feel part of the project, we try to have them stay with the team for the longest time possible.

How do the Design Technology experts at Heatherwick operate, and how do they interact with the project teams and outside parties?

PZ: As a studio, our own interests are related to understanding whatever surrounds us and whatever can become a design driver. It may not quite be the same as in other practices. Here, a lot of our influences come from making, the love for nature and craft. We come from a background of playing with materials, hence understanding material behaviour is key for us.

Within Digital Design, BIM, Immersive Media, and Ge-Code work together to optimise workflows and to support intuitive documentation, to maximise interoperability, and to ensure we can prototype and rapidly visualise what we are designing. For Ge-CoDe's applied research projects, we usually assign one person who will be leading the project with the external partner, and we'll check in regularly to monitor and review the status of its development.

Tell me about the interplay between Design and Technology from your perspective. At Heatherwick, is technology just a means to an end, is it a major driver of innovation and creativity?

PZ: The use of technology is not just a means to an end at Heatherwick, but it is part of our studio culture. We engage with technology from the very start of projects. We use it to explore design ideas, through sketch modelling, rapid prototyping, parametric modelling, and visualisation. As an example: the Vessel at NYC's Hudson Yards was designed using parametric techniques. Its geometry was derived from a grid on a flat sheet of paper that was used to build a parametric model based on U,V coordinates. We engaged with Adams Kara Taylor (AKT, the structural engineers) early in the design process, and we were able to collaborate in the development of the design through the use of shared parametric definitions. This was also key to inform the fabrication process.

▼ **Figure 2.20**

Heatherwick Studio: The Vessel at Hudson Yards, geometry of the viewing platforms.
© Dominik Holzer

PRACTICE INSERT: Heatherwick Studio

To facilitate these processes, the Ge-CoDe team has developed Grasshopper templates that are applied across the practice, and we consolidate a great amount of support material in the form of tutorials which are then shared with everyone in our studio intranet. Next to the tutorials, the internal communications platform contains 'Case Studies' about past and recent projects and explain how we delivered them We use it to update staff about upcoming talks (either by internal team or guests) where we cover all things related to digital design, computation, and fabrication. We have also developed our own Rhino plug-ins that help expand the functionalities of Rhino to work better at making, managing data, and documenting.

In terms of tool use – how are you facilitating the transition from initial sketching, your Rhino/parametric-modelling-focused approach to your delivery in Revit (or similar)/and AutoCAD?

PZ: In order to address workflow issues, we developed a tool called the Interoperability Decision Tree. It asks users what they are exporting from and what they want to achieve. It then allows them to add questions such as is this a one-off documentation process, or will there be several iterations and changes? Are there any specific processes to apply? The tool guides users through a series of steps that help them make choices about the most appropriate software and tool ecologies applicable on a project via interoperability workflows.

Rhino is our main design tool. Modelling happens in it from early stages all the way to construction. From Sketch Design onwards, we usually deliver drawings and BIM through Revit. We maintain the link between our design models in Rhino and our delivery models in Revit through our own Rhino. Inside Revit™ workflows and through other plug-ins like BEAM. We are also starting to deliver some pilot projects in Revit at concept stage. Because of the varied nature of our projects, from objects to city districts, some projects cannot be documented with Revit, in these cases we use our custom Rhino documentation tools and templates. We have also developed tools that allow us to incorporate data information to our Rhino models and enable level-based navigation and modelling, adding some basic level of BIM to Rhino, without the need of advanced knowledge of Grasshopper.

Fabrication is also incorporated in the design process, and teaming up with technology to enable partners is key. A good example of this is our Maggie's Centre in Leeds. There we use natural materials in combination with nature to create an environmentally friendly, home-like environment that simultaneously has expressive geometry and three dimensionality. Understanding the fabrication process and working with the fabricators (Blumer Lehmann) was a key factor in the success of the project.

▲ Figure 2.21

Maggie Centre, digital model of stair wall/roof, digital fabrication, and interior shot upon completion.
© Heatherwick Studio

Are you comparing notes across your studios, and how do you collaborate with others when it comes to advancing and applying Design Technology?

PZ: Digital Design and Making meets weekly. We cover all projects and initiatives. Within Digital Design, the Ge-Code team meets once a month to discuss progress on projects, talk about the tools we are applying, tools we are developing, and on-going collaboration projects. Those meetings are also used to inform everyone about 'cool stuff' and latest developments that have grabbed our attention (this includes information about events and conferences we should visit). We talk about what is next and what is needed in terms of training, tools, and support. The BIM and Immersive Media teams are also invited to these meetings, so we can make sure we are covering all areas of technology and interoperability.

What are the limitations of Design Technology use at Heatherwick? E.g., are there instances where Design Technology may obstruct rather than support great design?

PZ: We work at such a rapid pace at the earliest stages of a project, we care about generating sketches and models. Sometimes the impulse is to try to resolve how to build a specific sketch when all that is needed is to quickly advance that sketch into the next one. However, our computation skills have proven really effective to quickly develop form at early stages. There is always a delicate balance between 'quick and dirty' and 'thought through' modelling.

Sometimes, people who are very technology oriented can get fixated on a problem that may not be worth solving. I would say that is a challenge, but with Thomas leading the studio, we quickly resolve such an impasse and drive the designers in the right direction to move on and keep exploring ideas.

How does Design Technology at Heatherwick evolve over time, and how do you respond to this challenge?

PZ: Digital design as well as the studio changes constantly. We are always exploring innovative, effective, and efficient ways of achieving extraordinary design, using the present technology and exploring the future. To navigate this constant evolution, we have worked hard on scalability and adaptability. We have built a strong base set of digital tools and workflows that allow us to explore, visualise, and deliver design quickly and effectively. We built a good base of knowledge that is available through videos and an internal platform that anyone in the studio can access. We regularly bring in inspiring people from outside the studio, for talks that keep our eyes open to the future.

We use our studio design values to filter through the immense number of technological developments that are always happening and focus on the ones that align with us and can make a real impact in how we explore and deliver design. Technology that bridges between what we do digitally and physically, or that enables the use of high levels of tridimensionality with new materials, as well as the idea of Advanced Craft, have been part our research for the past years. We are now using Mixed Reality as part of our design and making workflow.

▶ Figure 2.22

Hololens, making a bamboo canopy in collaboration with Fologram.
© Heatherwick Studio

2.6   Project Support

The logical extension of Design Technology management on an organisational level is its impact on projects. Ultimately, this is where the most DT efforts are directed. As discussed in the previous chapter, requirements for technology support can change from one project to another, depending on a great variety of factors. Starting with the project size, type, and location, the level of Design Technology interaction also depends on the particular preferences of those running the job, the capabilities of other supply chain members, and particular clauses listed in the contract.

Interestingly, though, the way in which projects are designed and delivered is changing. Facilitated to a large extent by technology, the process of design is becoming more interactive. If, in the past, architects would come up with a concept, advance it, and ask engineers and the contractor to 'make it happen', we now see far more co-rationalisation and feedback from engineering and construction/fabrication experts being woven into the way design is advanced. Within a traditional work method of architects, the early Schematic Design phase was mostly about translating the functional brief while addressing aesthetic considerations; now projects have become more information intensive. Analysis of (e.g.) environmental sustainability and project cost generates key performance feedback to test a project's feasibility in the early design stages. This exploratory effort may start mainly in-house but becomes increasingly collaborative, likely involving the contractors and fabricators at a point where the design is still flexible. This, of course, offers clients a better product, but it also comes with the requirement to re-jig the workflow of designers and the dialogue with their collaborators. This is where DT choices play a pivotal role on the project level.

Design Technology for Early-stage Criteria Design

At the start of a project, it is mostly left to the architects to decide which technology/tools to use. When exploring the project's morphology, they are presented with various applications to address the distribution of spaces based on the functional brief, to come up with a captivating solution for the project's appearance and material choice, to test and validate environmental performance, or to manage cost in accordance with the project budget.

As Schematic Design progresses and ideas firm up, architects start to coordinate their efforts with other parties such as the structural or environmental engineers. For this context in particular, rule-based modelling approaches have enabled designers to change their project workflow in order to become more interactive with their engineering partners. In 2007, the AIA California Council presented their ideas about 'Integrated Project Delivery' and proposed to abandon the terminology 'Schematic Design' in favour of the term 'Criteria Design'.[21]

When combining parametric design with performance optimisation, models representing the project's underlying geometry are shared across the various players of the project team. If in the past engineers would clearly want to engage the design once it was fairly determined in order to avoid tedious repetition of their calculus-heavy activities, they now can minimise that effort via flexible modelling environments that tie in directly with their analysis and simulation tools. On a practical, project team level, this requires the management

---

21   Available at: http://info.aia.org/siteobjects/files/ipd_guide_2007.pdf (Accessed: 31 October 2022).

of Design Technology support beyond the architecture firm's boundary. It has become common for architects to share their Rhino/Grasshopper models with their engineering counterparts in order to advance the design. For this to work seamlessly, clear rules need to be established among the collaborating parties, who have the authority to change the project's geometry for whatever purpose. The DT expert on the architecture side is likely going to develop recipes (or a set of rules) jointly with his/her engineering counterpart on the project in order to set the boundaries for the setup of the parametric model or any other algorithmic investigation that are undertaken jointly.

The convergence between designing and testing starts to extend into manufacturing processes as well for those projects where close collaboration with the contractor and their subcontractors is possible. The production pipelines and associated tool ecologies do not come out of nowhere. The project lead (possibly supported by a Design Technology expert assigned to the project) needs to negotiate these processes with other collaborators and facilitate an environment of trust and mutual respect when introducing the parameters to be explored across the supply chain. Only then, with clear constraints defined for the exploratory process, can the team search jointly for interactive solutions. Within this flexible optioneering process, questions about design authorship and authority may emerge. Who 'owns/controls' the geometry? Who is responsible for the adequacy of the final solution found? How can the input of various parties be balanced whilst maintaining strong design-leadership from the architect?

During design development and in particular when heading into contract documentation, regular project milestones ask for the production of project design documentation in fulfilment of client requirements. This is where detailed structural and façade information is needed, as well as the inclusion of mechanical and hydraulic/plumbing systems, layout of electrical systems, and fire/essentials. Project information becomes increasingly determined, in preparation for the input of specialist contractors who ultimately determine the exact equipment or system to be installed.

This represents the next major challenge/opportunity for the integration of Design Technology into the project-based workflow. How can technology assist in the coordinated delivery of design documentation and potentially also offer direct links between the 3D topology models developed for design and the discrete, component-based fabrication process?

Visualisation Options – From Teaser to 'Work in Progress' to Final Output

Visualisation has always held a special position within architectural design as it is both a way for project teams to advance their ideas, as well as a manifestation of those very ideas. The reasons for producing visuals are therefore multifaceted. On a project level, they oscillate between visuals for office-internal (formative) and office-external (informative) purposes. Whereas the former acts as an essential driver of design ideas that help to communicate the current state of (parts of) the project whilst offering various alternative solutions, the latter tend to communicate the project as 'product' that allows it to be marketed to the client (or group of clients).

For many architecture practices, the shift towards producing engaging 3D images of their projects via computational means has reduced their dependency on hand-drafted axonometries or perspectives of their work. With their manually derived predecessors often seen as the key output of an experienced designer with 'a great hand', these representations can now be produced – in principle – by students or recent graduates with the right 3D skills. As much as hand-sketching remains a pivotal means of communicating design ideas on projects, computer-generated visualisations now represent a large proportion of graphic output on projects. The Design Technology team typically works closely with the office's visualisation experts to determine which type of output (still/moving/sketch-level/photorealistic/VR/etc.) is required for different stages on the project. Mapping this out upfront then helps determine how far visuals are to be generated by the project team itself or whether specialist support is required.

In some instances, where high-quality photorealistic images and/or animations are required, architecture firms outsource their production to specialist third-party visualisation firms. They have production pipelines set up to generate the desired output in a short amount of time and with the right expertise to turn out stunning visuals. This typically requires a liaison person on the project team to communicate the purpose and stylistic affordances of the required output. The third-party visualisation firms are heavily reliant on the 3D models they receive from the architects to advance and animate them towards captivating stills or animations. This means the architects need to be cognizant of the software interfaces between their tools and those of the external visualisation experts.

For lower-level in-house use, visualisation applications now include a great array of built-in settings that allow designers to produce high-quality visuals without requiring expert skills in texture mapping or animation. In addition, Virtual and Mixed Reality output can now practically be generated and accessed by anyone as associated hardware for immersive and interactive use of VR has become more affordable. VR thereby not only serves architects as a means to communicate design outcomes with the client, but it also offers decision support during the conceptual design stages. The advancement of visualisation does not stop there as features for representation and documentation tools converge. BIM models conceived for design documentation can be interfaced directly with visualisation and animation software. Connecting BIM authoring models with tools like Autodesk's Fuzor™ makes it possible to create bidirectional links between an interface for design representation and for documentation. For the first time, visualisation is not merely a representation of design intent; design itself can be changed in the visualisation environment, and the underlying documentation is updated. Naturally, the very same base BIM authoring models can be used for VR output as well.

Visualising design output only forms part of the equation, once design concepts have been sufficiently advanced and signed off by the client, design teams typically progress towards detailed design and documentation.

Moving Into BIM – DT for Documentation, Construction, and Beyond

The multidisciplinary spatial coordination part inherent to the transition from concept design toward project team involvement is most strongly associated to object-oriented BIM execution planning. This is where the Design Technology effort becomes a 'social' exercise where architects negotiate their planning with the input from several other parties simultaneously.

From a Design Technology perspective, the BIM specialists within the firm not only need to be enabled to offer assistance with this process from a technical/modelling perspective, but they also need to be knowledgeable about procedural particularities of a BIM-enabled workflow. What really counts here is their ability to interpret the BIM requirements listed in the client brief and their translation into actionable tasks and responsibilities of various supply chain members they interact with. Central to this process is the formation of a project-specific BIM Execution Plan that helps to orchestrate the collaborative effort across all parties. The BIM Execution Plan outlines the collaborative process in great detail and contains references to workflows and templates to be used by anyone on the project team who is working in BIM. The BIM Execution Plan has become essential for all medium- to large-scale construction projects as it ties together the tasks fulfilled by various supply chain members in BIM towards a joint delivery mechanism. BIM project support thereby expands from detailed knowledge about in-house modelling standards and documentation styles, all the way to the coordination of models across the entire team, plus the incorporation of any requirements listed in local policies or Client BIM Briefs. As part of that, modelling parameters and view templates are shared across the project participants to ensure consistency in the documentation output they produce.

A BIM representative within the DT team needs to be present in the project initiation phase to help determine the best way to support the project architect and other collaborators. This expands into conversations about skills and staffing. In some instances, additional BIM training for select staff may be required, and the BIM Manager is responsible for determining such needs and to follow up with the relevant training program. Additionally, the BIM Manager is also responsible to ensure that all project team members are complying with the in-house BIM/documentation standards as well as the use/creation of BIM objects in the office BIM library.

Once the multidisciplinary BIM effort on a project has started, it is the project's BIM Manager's responsibility to ensure that work is undertaken according to the project's BIM Execution Plan, fine-tuning the team's approach over time to incorporate any changes required based on client feedback or agreed-on project team preferences (e.g., when moving to the latest BIM authoring software version).

Initially focusing on the coordination of BIM efforts between architects and engineers, the BIM Execution plan then is extended to address the specific affordances of construction (and ultimately the facility managers).

In recent years, increased emphasis has been put on project teams working in BIM to export data from their models for use in facility and asset management. Here, Design Technology expertise is required to assist the project team members in appropriating their model output from BIM to align with the data input desired by the client's facility managers. In some instances, clear prescriptions of what data exactly the client wants to get out of BIM on a project is missing. It is therefore left to the lead designer at project initiation to seek clarification about the datasets to be exported from BIM for facility management (FM).

Once the project team has a good understanding of the data the client is after, they can adjust their modelling effort to include the relevant meta-data categories and/or find ways to automate the transfer of model information relevant for FM via a Construction Operation Building Information Exchange (COBie) schema. There, the project team assigns selection criteria for model data transfer and extracts project information into Excel™ files via COBie filters. In some instances and depending on client preference, the project team may use third party software to facilitate the COBie extraction.

Other than in small firms, it is rather uncommon for the project architect to act as the key BIM person on a project level. With a lot of hats on already, the BIM side is typically taken over by a dedicated and BIM-enabled staff member or by someone within the office who works in this role across several projects (supervised by a local BIM Manager). The project architect needs to decide what workflow pipelines are going to be used to transition from the construction documentation models/drawings to the construction/installation processes on site.

For Morphosis, moving fluidly across conceptual design and delivery has never been a major issue, as most of their staff are highly versed in different aspects of Design Technology. They manage to integrate them as a matter of course and with strong focus of bespoke affordances on any given project.

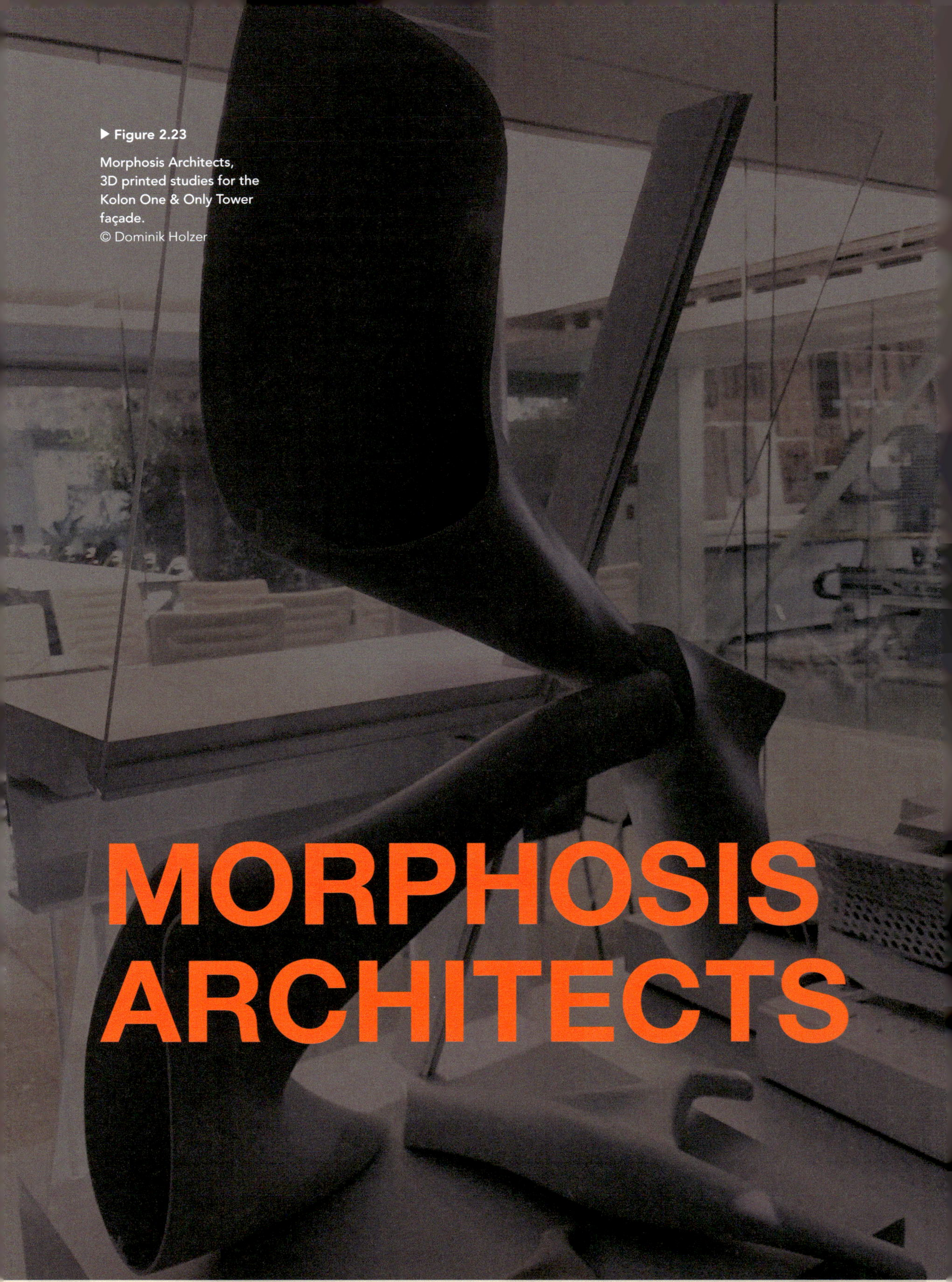

▶ Figure 2.23

Morphosis Architects,
3D printed studies for the
Kolon One & Only Tower
façade.
© Dominik Holzer

MORPHOSIS ARCHITECTS

Thom Mayne has been part of the transformation of architectural practice via digital means for several years. As the founding partner of Morphosis Architects and alongside others such as Frank Gehry or Eric O. Moss, he has been on the forefront of a design movement that keeps making a major impact on the local LA architecture scene (and beyond) since the late 1970s. With close ties to design and research at the Southern California Institute of Architecture (SCI-Arc, which he also co-founded), Mayne has shaped Morphosis over the years to embrace Design Technology as an intrinsic part of their design approach. Here, he is joined by their Director of Design Technology Kerenza Harris to share his views on making buildings (not drawings), 3D printing, BIM, and the 'synaptic stuff' that jumps across projects.

When writing 'Change or Perish' in 2006, you reflected on changes occurring in your practice over the previous fifteen or so years to then providing an outlook for the future. We are now fifteen-plus years on. How (relevant) do you see your comments from back then?

Thom Mayne (TM): I just read something that reminded me of that. It was an article about Amazon's founder Jeff Besos going through the history of starting the firm. Besos discusses when he was in the garage, having to sell books on Amazon, he had the idea of creating an online bookstore. He thought to himself: in this [market] climate, nobody is going to shop anymore, there is no reason for it. There are only two reasons people would still go to brick-and-mortar stores: Convenience (milk/toothpaste), or entertainment . . . and he got it! It was completely obvious that – with the impact of computation – the world was going to move in a certain direction. Personally, I was looking at a 'death warrant': I am absolutely technologically incapable. My brain is not wired mathematically. It definitively requires a kind of thinking that a mathematician or a physicist, who operates in this space, is going to have. I got through calculus and ended up fine, but when I took my first real math class in college, I blew it. I could memorise it, I could operate on a certain level, but I could never actually understand the complex formula we were dealing with. Yet it became obvious to me that this was going to be the future of our profession.

▶ Figure 2.24

Kerenza Harris and Thom Mayne in the office.
© Dominik Holzer

PRACTICE INSERT: Morphosis Architects   83

I have been interested in the development of ideas that are methodologically driven; they come out of a process – they are not 'a priori.' As a young man, I was very much influenced by Peter Eisenman and especially Bernard Tschumi. There was a time in the seventies and early eighties where the discourse centred around methodological means and operational strategies. That type of approach was producing work that is about combinatory, interactive behaviour. It was not about objects but the relationship of things. It made new things out of these relationships. That has been my focus for my whole life. When the computer came along, I recognised immediately that it gives me the simplest means for integrating these two 'things' – methodology and strategy. I was spending a week and a bit drawing this, and another week doing that; now, with the help of the computer, my staff can give me fifteen combinations in one hour. It became totally clear that the computer would take us to places in a design sense. That is where I am totally focused in looking at organisational strategies and notions of formal organisational ideas; everything after that is dialogue. The other thing is that I have always worked collaboratively. I am not a Lebbeus Woods or a Michael Graves. I work back and forth through conversation, even at the beginning of the ideas. The computer became obvious as a tool that glued everybody together.

In 'Change or Perish', you frequently refer to technology as a major impact factor, and you say, 'It is going to put us back as builders'. Has that happened?

TM: Not only has the digital world completely reconstructed architecture practice, but it is also going to move it forward even more so. We now have an office that sits approximately at one-third (these are numbers that probably mean nothing) of staff we would have if we still worked in a classical sense. One of the things that has changed radically from the classical process moving from schematic design to shop drawings is that we are able to 'jump over' the working drawing and instead manage to go right to the maker (the fabricator) in schematics.

▼ Figure 2.25

VR exploration on the office floor.
© Morphosis Architects

PRACTICE INSERT: Morphosis Architects

What role does Design Technology play at Morphosis?

Kerenza Harris (KH): In regard to the office tradition, technology has always been on the forefront, even when computers were not so evidently part of the workflow. There is a notion of construction and in-house investigations about materials and systems. The computer is a mark of technological advancement in society in general, and we use it for more than just a tool; it is very much part of the culture at Morphosis. At the office, technology is approached as a tool to realise ideas, and concepts – rather than driving the identity of a project, it functions as a 'means to an end'. It also allows us to keep ideas in play simultaneously. As an example: we have been using the 3D printer since 1999; it is fully integrated into the workflow in a way that does not seem like an add-on or tangent to the design process. In fact, we design specifically for interoperability with these tools, creating scripts and using specific formats in a way that communicates to the printer easily. We also acquire a lot of things – techniques, process, tools – from other industries, for example from gaming or immersive media.

▲ Figure 2.26
Kolon One & Only Tower (KFR), series of 3D printed working models for the project.
© Morphosis Architects, Image Credit: Jasmine Park

TM: One of the things that interests me about the technology we use is its potential to help us in reducing risk. In a traditional set of drawings, it is impossible not to miss certain coordination errors. In the model, the 2D outputs are automatically synthesised, so it radically shifts risk. If you look at the amount of change that we commit, and you look at the change orders, the use of technology is having a very interesting pragmatic effect. Throughout my entire career, we have been able to build what people perceived to be expensive, complicated buildings for very normative budgets. Technology has allowed us to practice in a way that allows us to experiment in what we are interested in under pragmatic, normative terms; we could have never done that without these tools.

How is Design Technology integrated at Morphosis on an organisational level?

KH: We all have strong personalities, but Morphosis is a truly collaborative environment and ideas come from all directions. On a daily basis, a team might be taking directions and exploring concepts from someone half our age. The way the company is set up, it's more flat – not so hierarchical. We are working together towards a common goal, and there is a certain level of fluidity about what the solution might be. As a medium-sized firm, we do have some structure for organisational reasons. We run the practice with four partners; each has their particular

PRACTICE INSERT: Morphosis Architects

area of expertise and global region of architecture. On the project architect level, we have staff with specialist skills who oversee Design Technology more generally or, for instance, BIM. Other, more general distinctions are for designers, project teams, and the fabrication shop, who create architectural models as well as prototypes, mock-ups, and even production for small projects.

It appears that the 3D virtual model now serves as the essential instrument to advance your design thinking at Morphosis.

TM: The model is now a collaborative tool, unlike a set of drawings we used to have where all of the mistakes were made. Across disciplines you looked at plan, section, elevation and detail . . . you had to take all these sheets and conduct checks on them. Drawings have hundreds of thousands of bits of discretional information on them; if you only get half a percentage wrong, you still end up with a lot of errors. The 3D model on the other hand becomes the communication device, and all your consultants look at the same thing – which is synthesised. It is the tool that is gluing us together.

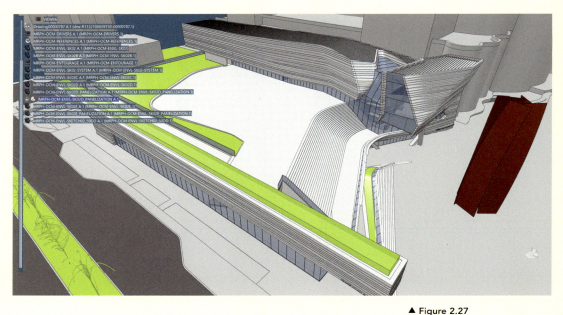

▲ Figure 2.27

OCMA CATIA BIM model screenshot.
© Morphosis Architects

We have seen that engineers are principally enabled to work in model-based collaboration, but some choose not to do that as it may add extra effort to their optimisation processes.

KH: For us, this model-based collaboration is a no-brainer, and we expect this from our engineers as well. This kind of integrated workflow is integral to the technologically facilitated design process I described earlier. What is really interesting, though, is that with the technology we have now, we are able to take detailing to a much higher state of resolution than ever before – we can participate in the collaboration with our engineers at a much deeper level. These applications have opened access to architects – they let us understand our designs in a technical way that previously was only available to specific engineering disciplines.

TM: We are known as a studio that brings in our consultants very early – it might even be prior to the initial forming of the job. Again, technology enables us to move at a certain pace; it is not just efficiency, it is allowing us to make intelligent decisions within a highly subjective context.

At Morphosis, is technology just a means to an end, a major driver of innovation and creativity, or somewhere in between?

TM: For us, the use of computation as part of our design process is not just about efficiency. Yes, it allows you to look at many more options in a shorter period of time; and I guess you could say, that is efficient. But the important thing is I could look at one thing and, in the past, I did not have the tool to do that. Now, it is a little bit like shifting from a slide rule to a Texas Instrument calculator. The digital technology we use increases our conceptual thinking abilities. With that, it expands the number of options. Any kind of creative process is discretionary. You put something down, you somehow think or feel, or look at it and change it; then you look at it again, and you change it again. It is a series of discretionary operations. With the computer, it just ramps it up to the power of ten! Now I can look at eight things instead of one or two things; it expands your creative world. The old hand-crafted models we used would take us a month to produce. Your brain just went 'daah'. Now with the 3D printed models, it is quite the opposite. If anything, it keeps up with your brain or is ahead of it, depending how you are working. It keeps you really alert. In any creative act, if it is music or writing, there is a certain intensity that you want to keep. With that comes the cross-pollination of ideas. With people who work collaboratively, inevitably some stuff is moving non-logically; it is 'synaptic stuff' that is crossing lines with one project influencing another.

How do you select your tool ecology on projects?

KH: The ecology of tools changes depending on the complexity of the project and the project phase. Most commonly, in early design phases we use software such as Rhino/Grasshopper and Bentley Microstation, which allow us to quickly iterate designs and rapid-prototype (either virtually or using 3D printers). Then we have a period of optimisation and rationalisation, during which we'll rely on powerful platforms like CATIA (Dassault Systèmes 3DEXPERIENCE). Historically, Bentley MicroStation has been the main software we have been using for documentation and delivery, though in the last few years we have begun adopting Revit, as many of our consultants are now communicating through that platform.

Do you have projects where you split your software use and work on the more regular elements in Revit/Bentley to then do more complicated elements (e.g., a delicate façade) in CATIA?

KH: In general, this happens on every project. First, however, we develop massing and basic forms – these are the underlying primitives that drive the overall design direction. This geometry gets shaped and formed through programmatic requirements, simulation, and other factors. Those masses are shared by everybody for further development; through CATIA, this becomes a parametric relationship. Revit is used for more orthogonal repetitive spaces, while the more complex areas are dealt with in CATIA and Bentley MicroStation while the design is still in process. CATIA is typically used for developing complex systems and geometries, such as façades, atrium areas, and other complex surfaces. At that point where the design is fixed, the project information gets inserted into Revit for documentation purposes. This workflow has been effective for us, but it does create interesting situations where, across platforms, some parts of the building are resolved while others are still in play.

PRACTICE INSERT: Morphosis Architects

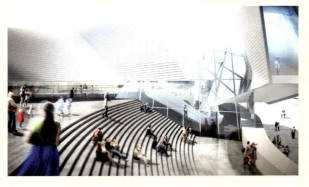 

▲ Figure 2.28
Render of OCMA project –roof terrace/OCMA project façade detail.
© Morphosis Architects

What are the limitations of Design Technology use at Morphosis? Are there instances where Design Technology may obstruct rather than support great design?

KH: Sometimes we have to be careful because Design Technology gives you a certain amount of power and a level of detail that may not always be good for us. You must be able to step away, look at the bigger picture, and not let technology push you. The more parameters you would add to objects or operations, the more you run the risk of narrowing down your options too early. Smart Models are hard to make flexible and creative. The smarter you are, the more defined you are, the less creative or flexible. Our expertise is to try somehow for both things to happen at the same time.

TM: It may be a generational response; I am classically trained, and the classical tools persist in the way I see design. I made the shift of understanding a plan or section drawing as a CT scan of the 3D model; cut it horizontally, and we call it a plan, et cetera. For me, the scan is still an important way of observing, and I demand a certain kind of elegance, a certain kind of quality in plans and sections that is part of this office. That would be different from the young people coming out of school for whom a plan or section is just an abstract. On a broader cultural level, one of the issues with technology is the way we make mistakes. The precision is difficult for me. The imprecision is important, usually in the earlier parts of a project. In any creative area, the mistakes end up being one of the most interesting parts of the process.

How does Design Technology at Morphosis evolve over time? Where would you like to see things going?

TM: I would like to condense the design process down from idea to construction as a singular act that bypasses all the traditional project phases. The first thing you show, some parts of it will be on a shop-drawing level, and some of it is still being worked on conceptually. The contractor steps back a bit, he is just an organiser; you go right to the people building the project. I am fascinated by the micro-macro way of thinking. You are using different parts of your brain and doing things simultaneously. You also become more pragmatic about which things you are working on. Some contractors are a little shy in terms of exploring or innovating; they are not ambitious in that sense. On the other hand, especially in Asian countries like Korea and China, you will work with somebody right now, and they initially may not have a clue what they are getting themselves into. But they will still say, 'I'll do it'. They will do it because they are progressive and want to be part of the cutting edge of the industry. It is an incredible time for the profession. Technology keeps pushing everybody to do buildings you could not have imagined a decade ago.

▶ Figure 2.29

Kolon One & Only Tower (KFR), Korea, façade mock-up.
© Morphosis Architects

▼ Figure 2.30

Kolon One & Only Tower (KFR), Korea, exterior view.
© Morphosis Architects Image Credit: Jasmine Park

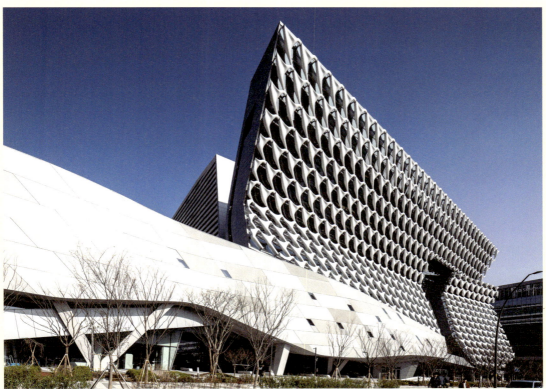

PRACTICE INSERT: Morphosis Architects

2.7 Design Technology: Liaising With Practice Leadership

As technology becomes increasingly engrained in ever more activities across architectural practice, it becomes pivotal for those looking after Design Technology to streamline their communication with decision makers within their firms. This is not only about ensuring they are informed about expected expenditures and associated budget requirements but also about making transparent how the firm operates and how technology is used to streamline workflows. Further – and this goes into considerations occurring on a project level – Design Technology leadership should be involved in conversations about staffing in order to determine the most appropriate level and timing of support.

The Design Technology Budget

Design Technology–related activities have often been seen as black-box 'necessary evil' expenses without the opportunity for decision makers to engage with the associated processes and expenses in greater detail. One key component of a successful liaison strategy with upper management is to establish a dedicated Design Technology Budget. In the past, the financial component of DT has often fallen awkwardly under the umbrella of Information Technology. This approach still seems to prevail in many design practices, but it bears certain risks. Firstly, Design Technology–related expenditure is by nature highly process dependent and therefore not simply associated to hardware/software or to networking cost. Secondly – and this is the key point – Design Technology management requires in-depth understanding of various facets of design. It thereby sits much closer to the core of what architects do than the skill sets required by IT experts.

If a separation between IT and DT budgets is a first important step, this needs to be followed by a detailed breakdown of expenses associated to various Design Technology support activities. Here it becomes relevant to draw a clear line between on-project cost and general overheads. When can the purchase of a new 3D scanner be costed against a project, and when is it more appropriate to cost it against the overhead budget? Does the Visualisation team sit within Design Technology, or is it a separate entity? How much money is available for in-house (or external) staff training in Grasshopper? Does the practice develop all BIM library content from scratch, or are there elements that can/should be bought from third-party providers? Is an R&D budget available that the Design Technology experts can tap into?

Project Data Audits for Upper Management

As we collect more and more information on projects, the resulting data leaves a trail of information that can be consolidated, cross-referenced, structured, and analysed. In doing so, practice leadership can extract valuable feedback that they use for decisions affecting projects and staffing. The information-rich environment of BIM promises to offer a repository of data that can be used to draw a far more detailed picture of staff/project performance. BIM tools allow for detailed data capture of time spent on any particular modelling/coordination effort and beyond. If that project data is associated to user behaviour, patterns of information can be extracted to determine the quality of the modelling process not only on individual projects but also across an office's entire portfolio. The data analytics options for this 'BIM health check' are open-ended and simply depend on a firm's preference in interpreting the information that is already sitting hidden in their BIM systems.

Commercial applications and services are now available to upper management that allow firms to grasp the most relevant datasets and visualise them in a succinct way for rapid decision making. BIMbeats™ has developed a tool that consolidates relevant data extracted from BIM/CAD applications into graphically explicit dashboards that offer a real-time window into a firm's Design Technology performance. The availability of the resulting audit trails represents a game-changer for medium- to large-scale firms as the otherwise seemingly elusive effort associated to BIM and associated technology becomes visible and transparent. Highly explicit graphs help practice leadership to understand how software use and project progress are unfolding. One key component of this approach is to maintain a live database that captures performance across a firm's entire portfolio in order to then make the information accessible (typically via a cloud-based system) to be queried via different output media and interfaces. The resulting feedback can be used to proactively address staffing on projects, highlighting any skill gaps within an organisation (or across the wider project team) so as to flag situations where further mentoring or training is required.

For those who do not wish to engage a third-party tool/service such as BIMbeats™, other interfaces between (BIM) modelling tools and data output for operational needs can be selected. This includes tools such as BIMlink™, ADSK's Dynamo, or custom-macro-based dashboards. For those instances, firms still need to develop their own schemas and data interfaces (using applications such as Power BI) to consolidate the process-related BIM information most relevant to them.

Measure the effectiveness of training

▲ Figure 2.31

BIMbeats dashboard for measuring the effectiveness of training.
© bimbeats

Understanding Capability/Programming Training

Next to analysing existing project data, firms can also use technology to check their staff's skill in a broad range of software applications. These assessments are necessary from time to time to be able to identify any skill gaps that might impact on individuals' or project teams' productivity.

Focusing predominantly on BIM tools, companies such as Knowledge-smart™ have developed an array of online tests that help firms to benchmark the skill levels of individuals or groups. Typically carried out as an online assessment, the resulting data can be queried in multiple ways to offer a comprehensive picture of in-house capability, as well as providing benchmarks of how a firm tracks in comparison with the industry average.

The software skill 'checking mechanism' also comes in handy when recruiting staff. Many BIM Managers and project architects share their frustration of being dragged into endless job interviews, only to find out that promising candidates are not suitable as they lack the required technology skills to fulfil their role. If a positive Knowledge-smart (or similar) test result becomes a prerequisite for any interview, such nuisances can be avoided.

Regular (e.g., biannual) staff skill assessment tools for design software use also make sense to verify the baseline knowledge over time and take necessary steps to ensure everyone in the practice is on the desired level for the role they fulfil.

2.8   The Next Level – Design Technology as a Business Opportunity

The final section in this chapter, dedicated to the integration of Design Technology on an organisational level, pushes its transformative potential toward new business opportunities and ultimately the change of architectural design practice overall. Some leading design firms demonstrate that highly focused Design Technology expertise allows firms to market the technology side of the design firm as a (separate) business stream. Architects can 'reinvent' their practice and carve out a niche for their business if they find ways to reposition their services with the use of technology. So-called New Tech companies are demonstrating how innovative supply chain management and information management systems can severely disrupt outdated procedures across a number of existing professions and industries. Design and construction are not immune to this threat. As much as the 'big takeover of New Tech' has not (yet) occurred, its presence should nevertheless trigger discussions among the architectural profession on its inherent challenges and opportunities.

When considering opportunities, the first thought coming to mind is society's increased appetite for data. Architects traditionally have the role as integrators of information across multiple disciplines. That position has become weakened by the emergence of different contract procurement models, the advent of the project manager, and an industry with ever increasing segregation into specialised sub-consultants and contractors. Design Technology offers architects an opportunity to regain some of that lost ground, but going back to a Master Builder role from two or three hundred years ago misses the point: the entire industry is changing, and so do the relationships between different parties working on the procurement, planning, design, engineering, construction, and operation of facilities. The way data flows across these processes and the way information is exchanged among the participating stakeholders are still largely based on a linear, 19th-century workflows. Design Technologists should realise the potential of using the information at their firm's fingertips to reconfigure how their clients procure and operate their assets (this is where CASE and later WeWork excelled in the 2010s).[22] They could think about new ways of engaging with the contractors and the tender packages they release to their specialist trades (Gehry's 'Request for Proposal'[23] procurement approach being a prime example here), or they could harvest building information inherent to recently delivered projects to then use AI to help predict detailed specifications (as well as the operational needs of future assets by a client).[24]

These are just some examples of the opportunities for design firms to diversify their offerings and translate their practices into a distinct market force. Overall, it appears that architects still focus too heavily on delivering 'a design' that then somehow gets realised by contractors and project managers and that is then operated and maintained by facility and asset managers on behalf of the client. The former process takes on average two to three years (or less depending on the project size), whereas many of the other activities mentioned are ongoing.

The most important step for this to happen is for upper management to have a clear vision about where Design Technology can take them, followed by the identification of the market niche(s) the firm is best positioned to fill. Stepping away from 'traditional' design as the core business towards a technology-centric suite of services is a difficult hurdle to master that requires an entrepreneurial mindset, a clear business plan, and the availability of the right skills to master the transformation.

As demonstrated in this chapter, Design Technology proliferation within architecture practice occurs most successfully when tied to different aspects of a firm's core business and the management structures in place. Many design firms still underestimate both the effort required to get their Design Technology setup right, as well as the potential benefits they could derive from its output. Some architects only slowly warm up to the opportunities inherent to integrating technology support into their workflow, as there exist cultural barriers and misconceptions about the way it may negatively impact their creative design thinking. Those who have been able to complement their 'design-flow' with matching technology support environments typically do so based on conscious planning and strategic alignments that cover different aspects of their operations.

Work by the Brooklyn-based boutique design firm SO-IL offers a perfect example of how a small boutique firm can take advantage of global supply chains, smart use of technology, and locally available workforce to realise unique projects. Thereby, they are able to 'punch well above their own weight', whilst remaining agile and innovative across different markets.

Following a view behind the curtain of SO-IL's operation, Chapter 3 of this book addresses the ever changing context of computational tools and techniques that support contemporary architectural practice.

---

22 Fano, D. and Davis, D. (2020) 'New Modes of Building', in *AD Architectural Design*, Vol. 90. No. 2, Wiley, pp. 32–39.

23 Tombesi, P. (2002) 'Involving the Industry: The Use of "Request for Proposal" Packages at Frank O. Gehry & Assoc.', *Architectural Research Quarterly*, 6 (1), pp. 77–87.

24 Available at: https://provingground.io/2019/03/19/the-evolution-of-minecart-and-opportunities-for-leveraging-bim-data/ (Accessed: 31 October 2022).

▶ Figure 2.32

Amant project, physical façade studies.
© SO-IL

SO-IL

As one of the younger, more up-and-coming practices presented in this book, SO-IL can boast an impressive array of commissions around the globe. Founded by Florian Idenburg and Jing Liu, the Brooklyn-based studio runs projects in North America, Europe, Asia, and Australia. One key aspect the young firm associates with Design Technology is agility – agility to customise tools to suit their design approach but also agility to streamline their supply chain globally to pick and choose the suppliers and workforce that best suit their operations. Senior Associate Ted Baab and Principal Jing Lui delve into the details of the firm's approach.

What role does Design Technology play at SO-IL?

Jing Liu (JL): We are not a practice that is invested in a specific goal-oriented 'tech' and say, 'This is the technology of the future,' or, 'If we kept developing that, what can we get from it?" Instead, we often say: "What are the things in the air, things that lie just beyond what can be realistically achieved at this moment"? If we step out there, immediately you have to be inventive about questions like who is going to be the fabricator, who is going to figure out the geometric logics, who are the experts that we can assemble around us to figure out how to break new ground? We leverage that desire to gather the project resource around it, and hopefully in every project, there is genuine new insight.

Ted Baab (TB): Nobody in this office provides tech support. We can always ask someone internally who can help figure out a hurdle or who has dealt with a similar problem before. In every project, technology can serve a different purpose. When you look around the office, we are doing things using draping or wrapping techniques. This design approach is not native to a tool like Rhino. Instead, we have come up with our own tools and modelling techniques using Grasshopper (some of which we have developed with geometric consultant Andrew Witt). We have been modelling this physically via a heat-shrink plastic to look at material behaviour rather than a purely geometric one. We still use the Grasshopper tool on several projects. We end up reinventing it a little bit each time, but the inherent processes allow us to explore different geometries with precision. This is an example of a design strategy that is not native to a digital tool but is facilitated by it. It allows us to use digital and physical models more interchangeably.

▼ Figure 2.33

Amant project, testing façade behaviour via digital and physical models.
© SO-IL

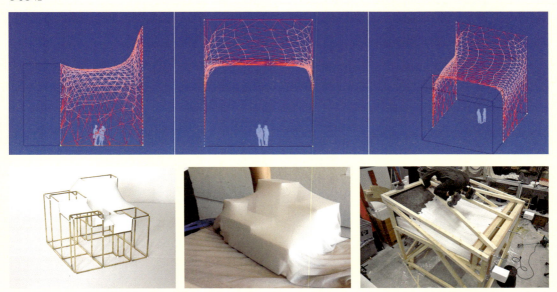

PRACTICE INSERT: SO-IL

With a studio of this size, I do not imagine you have your own DT team. Are there any management processes that you apply when it comes to technology?

JL: Indeed, we do not have a dedicated research or technology team such as with other bigger architecture practices. Research and innovation are part of the culture, and the projects are their platform. We very intentionally find ambitious projects and collaborators in those projects so in each we stretch ourselves beyond what we already know. Our research is through experimentation in real-life situations. Sometimes, dreaming up strange things and trying to materialise them is the best way to develop new tools and techniques.

TB: We frequently find an idea that we are interested in. We have to find a way to control and realise it, rather than working through a fascination with one technology or tool.

JL: Technology in our work is not a linear process. It is highly circumstantial and happens when we do things. For example, in one overseas project, the Kukje Gallery in Seoul, we tested a non-existent façade material in the computer with simulation first to determine the desirable behaviours. We then went deep into manufacturing land in China and found some skilled labour via Alibaba. They did not need to comprehend the intelligence behind the thinking and engineering, but their skills allowed us to make something that only existed in our head into reality.

▼ Figure 2.34

Kukje Gallery (Seoul), using STRAND to test the façade geometry's deflection from a minimal surface model.
© SO-IL

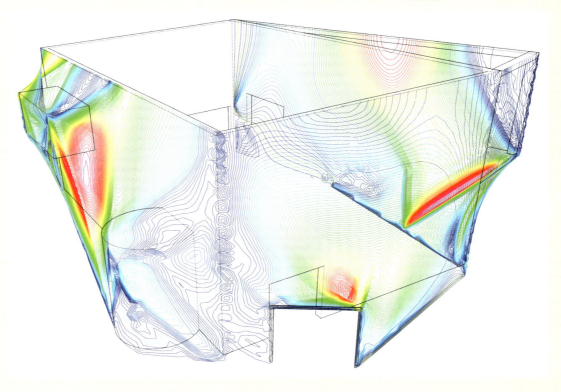

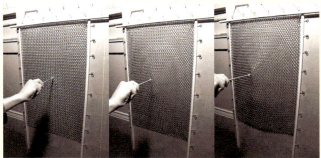

◀ Figure 2.35

Kukje Gallery (Seoul), mock-up/mesh stretching test/installation on site.
© SO-IL

Which management structures do you have in place to effectively apply Design Technology at SO-IL? Please mention human resources as well as hardware/infrastructure available.

JL: We try to incorporate it into our culture. For example, every intern or new staffer that comes through the door takes a crash course on Grasshopper, so they (re)gain the geometric control right on the first project they do.

TB: We use both Rhino and V-Ray™ heavily; they are our primary design tools, and we test everything through renders and physical models. Probably half of the office uses Grasshopper regularly.

Are there any cultural clashes?

TB: It is unfortunate that there is always a line that separates new technology as a skill instead of as a way of thinking. What sometimes seems to be merely a tool we can realise in hindsight is extremely informative on how we approach design. When I was in school, we all learned Grasshopper. Yet right now, none of our interns knew Grasshopper before joining us. For me, this is a problem. Familiarity with more than one tool allows us to see design problems using different terms. Yet at the same time it is not hard for new staff to learn new tools generally. It is interesting to see how technology grows up with different cohorts. For us looking back, these look like technologies, but for students in schools now, it is the way they learn to make architecture.

How do the Design Technology experts at SO-IL operate, and how do they interact with the project teams?

JL: We try not to have one dedicated person who looks after one specific tool/ environment of our work; this cuts across a range of different activities in our practice. We are a young practice; some people are good at using certain tools, and others are still getting there. We try to avoid having dedicated 'tech' people where one looks after Rhino and the other after BIM. Our BIM library is very much like an open-source project.

I am interested to hear more about how you collaborate with the fabricators and what you hand over to them. You mentioned your Alibaba project using labour from China, how did you interact with their local representatives?

JL: We have people on site who work with the fabricators closely. Naturally, our involvement depends on the sophistication of the fabricators. If the project budget permits, we work with sophisticated fabricators who preside over complex tools and machinery that seamlessly connect with our information. We can give them a Rhino or BIM model, and they can manipulate and appropriate it, to then go back and forth between us and them to get the best results. In a way, this process is very exciting. We often learn a great deal from them as they know their materials and tools the best. We are also quite open-minded about adjusting the original design intentions to incorporate new discoveries while working with particular fabricators. Unfortunately, not every project allows for that. Some projects you have to work in a highly manual way with people who sometimes do not even read 2D drawings. Then you have to sit next to them and work it out together.

TB: On more complex projects, it helps to have an intermediary who is from the fabrication side. A fabricator such as FRONT (with whom we work on several projects) facilitates fabrication-ready the shop drawings based on our Grasshopper model. They come at it from the other side.

▼ Figure 2.36

K11 (Hong Kong), fabrication machinery/installation/testing of bespoke glass columns.
© SO-IL

98   PRACTICE INSERT: SO-IL

I am taken by the fluidity about how this can happen these days and how 'fresh' your approach is to resolve these issues. Is tech just a means to an end or creativity or in between?

JL: It is both for us. In our generation of a practice, design processes are rarely linear, they are a great deal of back and forth and collaboration. We have to define at which point what technology is the most helpful on any given project. From the beginning, tools like Photoshop, diagrams, sketches help us to understand and advance the conceptual approach quite quickly, and then Grasshopper assists with our systematic thinking. The physical models are used for form finding and for understanding proportions. We do all of them in parallel at once.

TB: Both at once is very important. There is no linear (or top-down) way we go from one to the next. As a design process, the office is much more organised like a newsroom. Everyone comes up with ideas, and then we talk about them like editors. We are not waiting for a sketch that we then execute. Everyone will do sketches, everyone will come up with ideas, everyone will find references. These inputs all arrive at once and become the basis for discussion.

JL: Senior people act more like editors and provocateurs. The younger generation is encouraged to participate in the conceptualisation of the projects. We also try to engage them in the conversation with our collaborators and ask: 'How are we actually going to make this? What is the thing we are trying to push hard here?' If we dwell in our computers for too long, we are then not engaged with the limitations in the real world, so we remind them to get out. That is something that is very important in our office: every project needs to have enough 'tension' with the real world.

In terms of tool use – how are you facilitating the transition from initial sketching, your (assumed) Rhino/parametric-modelling-focused approach to your delivery in Revit (or similar)/and AutoCAD?

TB: Every project uses Rhino, and many use Grasshopper. There is a willingness of almost everyone in the office to try out new tools and processes, even if they are not familiar with them yet. We started using Grasshopper and associated tools not for their stylistic output but for the way they make us work more intelligently and systematically. For example, with a concert hall design, when we were discussing with an acoustical engineer, we could change the dimensions and proportions of the room on the fly. All the critical relationships of our geometry were set, but the parameters are all flexible. We were able to factor several performance constraints into our model and get real-time feedback.

You hence advance your projects in Rhino/Grasshopper and take them into 2D AutoCAD at some stage for documentation?

TB: That is how we typically document projects we do in-house, but more projects are also being developed from the beginning in Rhino and Revit as well. The Revit process is newer to us but already has opened up new opportunities to integrations with Rhino and other tools later in the documentation process.

▶ Figure 2.37

Manetti Shren Museum (Davis–California), virtual 3D curvature analysis model/metal façade-panel mock-up.
© SO-IL

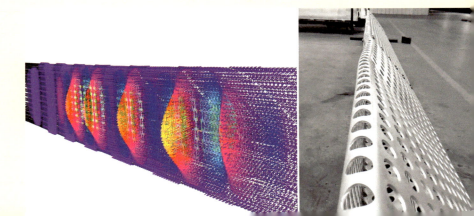

How is BIM positioned across the practice more generally?

JL: Until now we have been designing with other tools to a certain point, to then translate our designs to BIM in the delivery stage. I think more and more we will be using BIM from early on.

TB: That has primarily been on larger projects where we have been working with another architect. Usually, bigger architectural firms almost exclusively use tools like Revit. For example, the Davis project was entirely in Revit. Our design studies and design development were primarily through non-BIM tools such as Rhino and V-Ray. Now, many of our projects are developed and documented more in parallel using Revit while we still break out portions to study in Rhino.

Are there any limitations to the Design Technology use in the practice?

JL: We sometimes feel that while BIM helps to make a project 'real' quickly, it might be too quick in some instances. If you know too much about the individual parts of the building, you might miss the big picture. It becomes rigid too quickly.

Are there instances where Design Technology might obstruct rather than support your approach?

TB: The limitation is probably more Rhino; it can become dominant, as many staff members work exclusively in it. The benefit of switching to physical models is not that we do not have the skills to do something in Rhino but that Rhino may obscure the way we are seeing something or thinking about something.

JL: I will give you a specific example: We were recently exploring the structural and formal logic of a concert hall project by pulling points in the Rhino model. But since it is not bound by physical properties, the forms being studied did not feel right. We then switched to studying it in a physical model. As soon as we did that, the form emerged naturally. Even if one is very skilled in modelling software, it is another medium. It takes translation from the virtual to the physical and vice versa, and in that translation, something is lost or misaligned. So it is important to do both simultaneously.

How do you see Design Technology evolving for you?

JL: There are a few interesting strands. One is the use of robotics in construction. It will expand some possibilities and limit others in our buildings. I believe that Artificial Intelligence is also an interesting development. Currently, AI is not interacting with the design profession that much, but I am 100% sure it is going to develop, and maybe one day we will design together with an AI.

TB: Almost every new layer of technology we integrated into the office, we have not expected or asked for. There are exciting new things we are interested in, and we try them immediately. Almost every time we bring in new technology or techniques, we find ways of working with that which gives us new insights about a project. Over the last few months, we have implemented a VR centre. It gives us completely different input on understanding scale and immediately jump from a sketch to a building you can walk into in a way that is unplanned. Each new tool, of course, has its limits but offers new freedoms as well.

▼ Figure 2.38

Manetti Shren Museum (Davis–California), digital curvature analysis/metal-mesh components.
© SO–IL

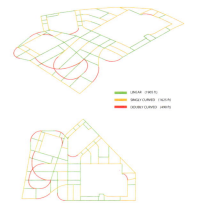

Chapter 3

Tooling

Having defined Design Technology in Chapter 1 and positioned it within design practice in Chapter 2, here tools take centre stage. How should design firms select them? What influences choices on projects? Are tools helping to determine process, or is it the other way round? In his 2009 article 'Thinking in BIM',[1] Bill Mitchell, one of the leading design and technology commentators, highlights the crucial relation between designers and their tools. According to Mitchell, there undeniably exists a bias between the tool, the tool maker, and the designer, with one influencing the other as a matter of course.

3.1 Seeking Alignment Between Design Process and Tools

Architects typically develop their design approach over many years, often linked to personal habits, extensive experimentation, and vocational training through ongoing practice. By nature, designers seek alignment between their desired exploration/production processes and the tools they apply. If they simply rely on processes that worked in the past, they run the risk of missing opportunities to innovate; if they push their experimentation with new tools too far, they run the risk of being taken out of their comfort zone or, even worse, failing to meet tight project timelines imposed by the client. This is where the rapid change in technology (as much as it can be seen as an opportunity) can become problematic. One continuously needs to question which tools to use, at what point in the design/delivery process, and how one tool might interface information from itself to numerous others. Ideally, designers can rely on a support infrastructure within their firm to assist with this challenge.

Those managing the rollout of Design Technology in practice require good oversight, not only about what tools are currently available but also about where these tools fit exactly within desired processes and the associated spectrum of software applications used in the firm. A basic understanding of how various tools emerged (and why), complemented by a good sense of where they are headed, offers a good starting point. Knowledge about how to expand on the standard features within a tool via scripting or programming becomes essential if further productivity improvements or design exploration avenues are desired.

---

1   Mitchell, B. (2009) 'Thinking in BIM', in *Architectural Transformations via BIM*, A+U Publishing, Tokyo.

Architects' ability to control the functionality of their computational design tools has undergone major fluctuations over the past four to five decades.[2] As discussed in the historical overview, the first digital design software applications were developed by a small group of design firms who purposefully crafted their tools to fulfil specific tasks. Since the advent of the PC era, tool development and distribution has increasingly become commercialised and focused heavily on off-the-shelf applications for mass markets. Computer Aided Architectural Design (CAAD) became a distinct field, as software providers marketed their tools as standalone applications their Application Programming Interface (API), making it difficult for common users to write their own scripts to expand on the standard features of the software.[3] Users started to become more dependent on the suite of functions offered by the software package they bought; anyone wanting to customise their tools likely required good scripting knowledge (and patience).[4]

Throughout the 1990s and early 2000s, large CAD and visualisation software developers (such as Autodesk, Bentley, Tekla, or Adobe) expanded their pallet of tools either via applications created in-house or via acquisition and incorporation of smaller developers/competitors. This approach was followed by an increased focus on consolidating those tools into suites or bundles of several (connected) tools, and it ultimately evolved into a subscription-type model with software being downloadable from online servers or running in the Cloud.[5] The subscription model (which is still the predominant approach today) locks customers into a perpetual cycle of annual software (version) updates. Many design firms have become dependent on the standard features of such tools/suites, which only get advanced via minor annual updates. Adding custom scripts to these prepackaged software solutions is possible, but it is mostly reserved for highly proactive and computationally advanced design practices that invest substantial time and effort in customising their suite of applications (predominantly in the BIM space).

McNeel's (the developer of Rhino/Grasshopper) approach offers a counterpoint to the fencing-in of applications as previously described. They promote a culture of peer-to-peer support, custom plug-in development by third-party users, and sharing of solutions across a wider community of users. In doing so, they facilitate the proliferation of plug-ins and schemers that allow designers to analyse a broad range of issues related to performative aspects of their projects. The more 'open-access' and peer-to-peer support nature of McNeel's Rhino/Grasshopper applications provides design firms a welcome balance between bespoke entry-level support and the ability for 'common' users to expand on those for their custom needs. For a great number of desired applications or 'effects', the Grasshopper/Rhino plug-ins offer a platform to pick from, hack into, combine, break, and reassemble in order to suit the needs of architecture practices.

Among globally leading practices, a community of users and contributors has emerged surrounding the proactive engagement with computational design tools and resulting plug-ins. Their technology specialists frequently compare

---

2   Mark et al. summarise eight approaches to design using CAD software in greater detail: Mark, E., Gross, M. and Goldschmidt, G. (2008) 'A Perspective on Computer Aided Design After Four Decades', *Architecture in Computero: Proceedings of the 26th eCAADe Conference*, Antwerp, 17–20 September 2008, pp. 169–176.

3   McCullough, M. (2006) '20 Years of Scripted Space', in *Programming Cultures: Art and Architecture in the Age of Software*, AD – Architectural Design, Vol. 76. No. 4, pp. 12–15.

4   This development was discussed in greater detail in Koutamanis, A. (2005) 'A Biased History of CAAD', *23nd eCAADe Conference Proceedings*, Lisbon, Portugal, 21–24 September 2005, pp. 629–637.

5   Martyn Day described a pivotal moment in the change of AutoDesk's business model in 2013. Available at: https://aecmag.com/news/autodesk-evolution/ (Accessed: 31 October 2022).

notes and put their heads together to share some of their approaches or even scripts developed in-house. Use cases for this flexible engagement between desired process and matching digital applications go far and wide: From geometry exploration, performance analysis, documentation support, fabrication, all the way to data analysis and AI. At times, architects aim to cut out the intermediary and go straight from file to fabrication or simply virtually test the boundaries of bespoke building materials.

3.2 Tool: From Drafting Support to Decision Support (and More?)

Ever since the start of computational design, those developing digital tools for architects envisaged for the computer to become an active partner in the design process. Early commentators such as Nicholas Negroponte (1970),[6] Chuck Eastman[7] (1975), or Nigel Cross[8] (1977) envisaged for humans to have conversations with computers, a machine that possesses the ability to handle ambiguity or inconsistency inherent to design thinking. In his essay on 'Architecture Machines', Negroponte pushes this notion furthest by stating that the support received from computer systems therefore needed to be 'very personalised' to allow both user and machine to (politely) interrupt the routine work of the other.

In retrospect, this utopian view of the intimate relationship between designers and their machines from the 1970s did not materialise on a broader scale in architecture practice. When considering the majority of tools assisting design, the interaction can (still) better be described as a one-sided monologue, with humans entering commands for the computer system to execute. The desired 'dialogue' or even conversation did not transpire initially, as computers appeared to be too 'dumb' and too slow to offer useful 'advice' within the fast-moving design process.

Without doubt, digital applications have dramatically increased productivity in architectural drafting and visualisation. They expand the architect's design capabilities and increase connectivity with project partners such as the engineers or the builders. Still, most off-the shelf applications rather represent a black box that offers little in the way of design decision support or even 'design agency'.[9] The potential for change is tied to architects' wider access to and adaptation of generative algorithms that help automate both quantitative and qualitative design feedback. Looking into the future, Negroponte's initial thoughts may prove to be not that illusionary after all.

Plug-ins such as Grasshopper's Galapagos allow architects to consider aspects of their design that can easily be quantified and then derive feedback from automated optimisation processes on what solutions perform better than others.[10] In simple terms, single-parameter optimisation can be achieved via

---

6 Negroponte, N. (1970) *The Architecture Machine*, MIT Press, Cambridge, MA. https://mitp-arch.mitpress.mit.edu/the-architecture-machine

7 Eastman, C. (1975) 'The Use of Computers Instead of Drawings in Building Design', *AIA Journal*, 63.

8 Cross, N. (1977) *The Automated Architect*, Pion Limited, Billerica, MA, p. 107.

9 Burry, M. (2011) *Scripting Cultures, AD Primers*, John Wiley & Sons, Hoboken, NJ, p. 14.

10 Johan, R., Chernyavsky, M., Fabbri, A., Gardner, N., Haeusler, M.H. and Zavoleas, Y. (2019) 'Building Intelligence Through Generative Design – Structural Analysis and Optimisation Informed by Material Performance', *Intelligent & Informed – Proceedings of the 24th CAADRIA Conference* (Haeusler M., Schnabel M. A., and Fukuda T., eds.), Victoria University of Wellington, Wellington, New Zealand, Vol. 1, pp. 371–380. Available at: http://papers.cumincad.org/cgi-bin/works/paper/caadria2019_104

this process, resulting in solutions that can enrich a designer's decision making. Autodesk, as one of the global market leaders in software development for designers, have recently launched their Project Refinery™[11] application (now titled Generative Design) that ties into their Revit modelling environment via their visual scripting interface Dynamo. After decades of use by researchers and Design Technology experts, the point seems to be reached where Generative Design will become mainstream across architecture (and engineering) practices globally.

The Generative Design tools described thus far typically require users to proactively configure the analysis parameters, whilst allowing for open-ended exploration of constraints.[12] The next step in the 'evolution' of Generative Design tools targets specific functions that occur in architectural design via a set of built-in utilities. One such tool is TestFit™, which allows users to evaluate site feasibility and spatial syntax/layout options based in variable building typology. Users can intuitively manipulate floorplan layouts whilst AI-supported algorithms (running in the background) offer real-time options for functional subdivision of apartment/workspaces, stairs, lift shafts, elevators, corridors, and balconies. One can generate complex floorplates on the fly, no matter whether investigating optimal carpark layouts or the 3D distribution of apartments. What sets TestFit apart from other tools is that it allows for a high degree of automation in site utilisation planning, whilst offering users to interact manually with the results as per their needs.

The use of Generative Design tools in everyday practice needs to be approached with caution: with architectural design depending on multiple inter-dependent factors from varying (professional) backgrounds, the single-parameter approach is limited. Here, multi-criteria optimisation algorithms such as Pareto-type solvers offer a more fitting solution to evaluate criteria on a broader scale. Grasshopper's Octopus is a tool facilitating such an approach, as it allows multiple, often conflicting parameters to be brought into context with automated routines to determine and represent a range of solutions that are better than others. The process of multi-criteria optimisation is still new to architecture practice, and not every designer will be comfortable in making decisions based on its use, let alone allow other professions to include their design criteria.

Parallel to developments related to performance feedback via analysis and simulation, Machine Learning (ML) applications using Neural Networks promise to offer additional feedback to designers, where self-learning (or semi-directed) algorithms are able to detract solutions based on precedence.[13,14] For example, Microsoft offers users a cloud-based ML studio via MS Azure™.[15] It centres on a visual authoring environment to develop data science work-flows via a web-browser interface, with no software installation required. Users can create R-scripts and draw on existing libraries (using R programming language for statistical computing) and do not even require specific coding skills. In some areas within the built environment, AI is already heavily in use, for example via Autodesk's Spacemaker tool[16] that helps planners explore

---

11 Available at: www.autodesk.com/solutions/generative-design/architecture-engineering-construction (Accessed: 31 October 2022).

12 Available at: www.generativedesign.org/ (Accessed: 31 October 2022).

13 Bernstein, P. (2022) *Machine Learning: Architecture in the Age of Artificial Intelligence*, RIBA, London.

14 Leach, N. (2021) *Architecture in the Age of Artificial Intelligence: An Introduction to AI for Architects*, Bloomsbury Visual Arts, New York/Camden, UK.

15 Available at: https://studio.azureml.net/ (Accessed: 31 October 2022).

16 Available at: www.autodesk.com/products/spacemaker/overview?us_oa=dotcom-us&us_si=4d4ce8c1-c707-428a-9bc9-813155019632&us_st=spacemaker&us_pt=SPCMKR (Accessed: 31 October 2022).

complex site characteristics and optimise the programming and use mix within a given site context. Increasingly used by developers and planners alike, the tool offers a data-driven decision-support environment in the master planning phase of a project.[17]

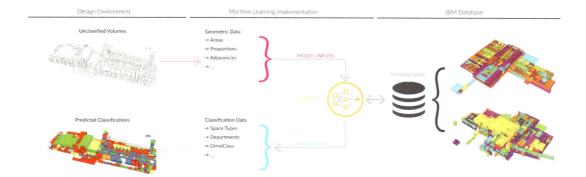

▲ Figure 3.1

Machine Learning workflow.
© Proving Ground

With Machine Learning showing promise of widespread adoption in coming years, architecture practice appears to be at an interesting crossroads: now that Generative Design tools are on the cusp of becoming mainstream, what kind of dialogue is it that we ultimately desire with computers? Who will ultimately be seen as the author of any particular design? Critical commentators voice their concerns about the seductiveness of tools over process. The fact that countless options can be analysed does not mean they should be. When architects draw on their feedback from digital tools and automation processes, what is the desired etiquette of their inclusion? How can this be approached, not from the perspective of a single individual communicating with a machine, but from the perspective of multiple design experts tossing around ideas and checking/evaluating their suitability on the fly, with computing as an essential contributor to this process?

To address such concerns, practices need to learn how to balance their desired design approaches with computational decision support. Design team members cannot be expected to possess the skills necessary to do so. It is therefore up to Design Technology leadership to map out and implement procedures that facilitate such dialogue across project team participants (the computer included). The Design Technology team needs to work jointly with the project teams in evaluating a firm's desired approach and develop bespoke solutions that offer the best cultural fit for their practice. In that sense, the interplay between human-led and computer-assisted design becomes highly personal with the potential to offer practices a distinctive market position.

---

17 Available at: www.spacemakerai.com/blog/how-spacemaker-helps-maas-partner-envision-future-working-environments (Accessed: 31 October 2022).

▼ Figure 3.2
The Londoner, collaborative work on the façade with artist Ian Monroe.
© Woods Bagot

For certain firms, Design Technology becomes essential to facilitate, streamline, sometimes homogenise design and delivery approaches across the various markets they operate in. With seventeen studios spread across six regions, Woods Bagot clearly falls under this category. When Shane Burger was initially recruited for his (present) role as Global Leader – Technical Innovation, the position was advertised as 'principal-track', meaning that the firm was clearly aware of its strategic relevance. Several years in, Shane helped transforming Woods Bagot via strong Design Technology leadership. The affordances of working across different markets and types of projects have resulted in Woods Bagot making highly conscious decisions about tools and tool infrastructures.

What role does Design Technology play at Woods Bagot?

Shane Burger (SB): The practice is very open and collaborative because we are a global company. Because we are not a signature name firm, we do not have a single aesthetic. We are a matrix organisation and a big aspect of this larger innovation community is about collaboration, sharing, teaching, and helping. You end up having people from three separate studios simultaneously working on the same project, and they all bring different expertise to bear, as well as different ways of working. We use communication and management tools like Slack or Teams, Trello, and Miro™ to manage project communications.

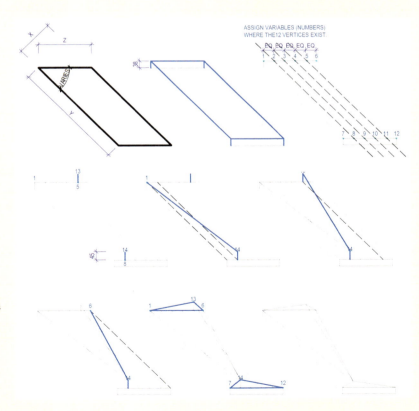

▶ Figure 3.3

The Londoner – digital models developed cognizant of fabrication method/glazed panels after firing/assembly models with structural engineers – prototype down to the connection detail.
© Woods Bagot

PRACTICE INSERT: Woods Bagot

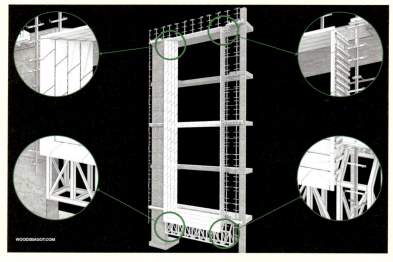

◀ Figure 3.3
(Continued)

How is Design Technology integrated at Woods Bagot on an organisational level?

SB: We organise our efforts globally with what are called 'Streams'. They exist in some form on every project and across the organisation globally. We have a stream called 'Client', another called 'Design & Delivery', 'Management', 'People & Culture', and 'Technical Innovation (TI)'. Design & Delivery focuses on the product of the work across the life cycle – everything from project establishment to concept and into delivery. TI focuses on the processes used to generate that product. We have members of that group in every region, every studio, and a wider community. In addition to overseeing that group, I lead a core research and systems development team called Design Technology. Our Design Technology team is mostly made out of trained architects, or at least architectural

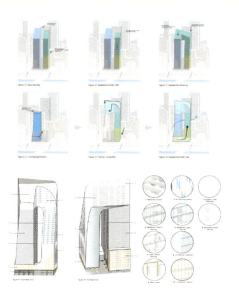

▲ Figure 3.4

447 Collins – collaboration with SHoP architects. Collaborative Revit model developed between two firms (W-B and SHoP) and two geographic locations (Melbourne and New York City).
© Woods Bagot and SHoP

technicians who know how to deliver projects. In the end process and product, TI and Design/Delivery, are very tightly knit. The Design & Delivery team is product focused, with an emphasis on concept, optioneering, project reviews, technical translations, building and material systems, constructability, etc. The TI group is taking all that Design & Delivery approach to then address the platforms and standards that sit underneath it – BIM, parametrics, and computation. Design Technology has become the lead, overseeing the requirements and the environment, and IT is supplying infrastructure and facilitation for the directions that are set by Design Technology.

Which management structures do you have in place to effectively apply Design Technology at Woods Bagot?

SB: The Design Technology community can be thought of as three groups: We have a global team that handles core resource development (content libraries, reference materials, etc.), platform testing (researching and testing the next generation tools, support and training, and so forth), and software development. The second group are the Design Technology leads in every studio. That role encompasses a mixture of project support, strategic development, and local R&D relevant to their market and studio. The third group is our in-house innovation community; it is effectively a user group of people who are talking about technology. A lot of times the conversations centre around platforms, like Rhino/GH and Revit. Increasingly we are exploring a larger ecosystem conversation around people using multiple tools and how they link – interoperability. Visualisation and VR, plus the use of Augmented Reality as it connects to either (Rhino/Revit) tool, becomes part of that broader conversation, as does the analysis methods we run on projects.

PRACTICE INSERT: Woods Bagot

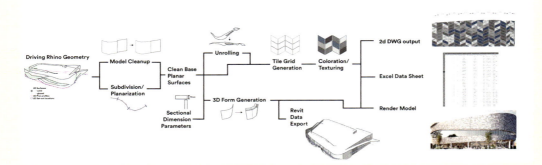

▲ Figure 3.5

Map of the design-to-delivery workflow – 'designing the design system' – mapping inputs and outputs spread across multiple tools for the Te Pae Convention Centre (Christchurch, New Zealand).
© Woods Bagot

I can imagine that keeping Design & Delivery apart is easier from a cultural perspective.

SB: I see cultural clashes a lot less so than a few years ago. In the past, there were senior design staff at Woods Bagot, and nobody had ever told them how technology could be synthesised into giving them the outcomes they wanted. Not just the outcomes but things they did not even know that were possible. When informed about the opportunities Design Technology afforded, it was a whole new ballgame. It became a conversation around digital craft (which is a term we use quite often at Woods Bagot) and not simply about software. What we want to talk about is all the extra stuff that you get as a designer: the ability to visualise things, the ability to go through multiple different schemes in a short amount of time, to be an augmented designer who is now provided with analysis and extra information, so you are better informed.

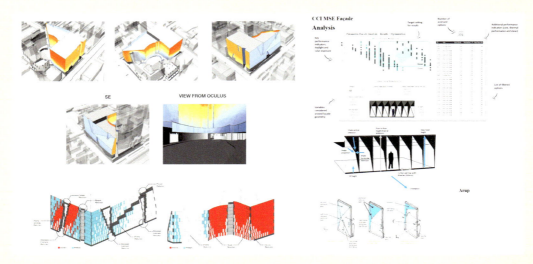

▲ Figure 3.6

Melbourne Connect – collaboration with Arup for façade performance modelling and panel shape scripting.
© Woods Bagot

PRACTICE INSERT: Woods Bagot

Among the people who sit more on the delivery end, the technical designers, I must admit that conversation was more difficult. They are used to their drawing sets and typical approaches to drawing markup. Getting them to break out of that mindset towards embracing model-based design reviews was a challenge.

How do the DT staff operate? How does the team get involved on projects?

SB: We get requests coming in for one of two things: it is either firefighting for something major that comes up from a project team or opportunity driven, coming from our design leadership. We have a problem, can someone help? That request will either come to me or directly to one of my team members, or it will bubble up from project staff. Resolving such an issue may require one of my team members to assist, or, if we know that another studio has capability (we try and stay as tapped into this as we can), that studio will then help out. Sometimes a request will come from a project team member directly. The second option is when we start a new project, and there is an opportunity to utilise Design Technology to try something new and interesting. In those instances, we aim for globally significant, portfolio calibre work . . . the best things we do.

At Woods Bagot, is technology just a means to an end, is it a major driver of innovation and creativity, or somewhere in between?

SB: I see two things we aim for in particular when it comes to Design Technology at Woods Bagot. One is it needs to be overseen as an overall robust core in terms of how we deliver our project work – making sure Design Technology is helping us to efficiently and consistently put our deliverables together.

The second part is that Design Technology and the overall technical innovation conversation are here to provoke our design leadership and to show them new methods of thinking. That includes everything from geometry, analysis, and visualisation, but also even in the conversations about new ways of structuring project teams, collaborating and workflows like Agile and Scrum.[18] It is about new processes and technologies. Our design leadership is focused on the product of the work, and Design Technology helps to oversee the process. This includes an innovation thread that is thinking two to five years in advance. I found that Design Technology has quickly moved out of simply being an IT support group, and it increasingly supports the disruption role.

In terms of the transition from design geometry into BIM tools, are you starting to become fluent in linking your Rhino files into Revit?

SB: To a degree, we are still faced with challenges on this front as we are dealing with a lack of interoperability and platform silos. When moving from Rhino to Revit, one needs to add a whole lot of semantic information in order to have a viable model in Revit. A lot of times it is still about bringing in references you build on top of. Sometimes it is about literally bringing it in and converting it to Revit-native geometry. You get to a point where you start having to add layers of meta-data to turn Rhino geometry into BIM objects. I do not know of any clear way of doing that. We have been speaking to Jon Mirtchin at Geometry Gym about using IFC as a translator.

Dynamo is not really solving the issue of linking an open, parametric design tool (like Grasshopper) to Revit. It is only good in automating certain aspects of Revit tasks. It has geometric capabilities that pale in comparison to

---

18 Available at: www.cprime.com/resources/what-is-agile-what-is-scrum/

PRACTICE INSERT: Woods Bagot

▲ Figure 3.7

The Eleventh, collaboration with BIG Architects. Mapping structural design with façade forms to autogenerate window and panel locations dynamically/developing a resilient workflow able to absorb frequent design changes and still product buildable documents.
© Woods Bagot

what Grasshopper does. It is frustrating for me to see people practically replicating tools and systems in Dynamo that we use in Grasshopper five times faster. We are finding that most of our staff who are using Dynamo are prototyping automation tools. Part of what I want to do with the software development team is to take those prototypes 'pro'. In that manner Dynamo becomes a Revit tool prototyping system.

The way Design Technology finds its way on a project is presumably quite different wherever you are located. How can you transfer knowledge between regions and studios?

SB: We are one global entity as a financial entity and as a shareholder base, so everybody benefits when everybody else benefits. There is a baseline understanding that our design leaders are all part of a collaborative group that does peer reviews of each other's projects.

▼ Figure 3.8

Melbourne Connect, brick façade scripted to drive assembly instructions for the bricklayers.
© Woods Bagot

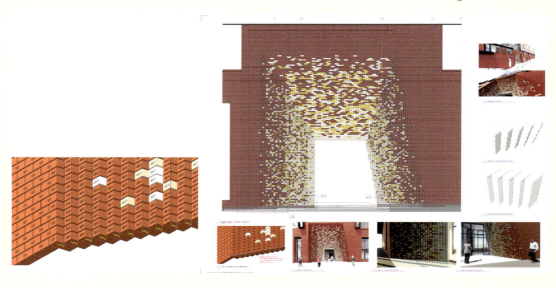

112   PRACTICE INSERT: Woods Bagot

▼ Figure 3.9

Melbourne Connect, façade under construction and close-up of panels.
© Woods Bagot

We are providing our designers, across all our studios, consistency in tools and methods. This helps ensure we can speak the same delivery languages, learn from each other, and riff off each other. This approach is particularly relevant once things get more consistent in the later project phases because typically the delivery (Revit world) gets more consistent. That said, we have a lot of sectors in a lot of regions that have very different market expectations. Our retail work in Hong Kong is different to our retail work in London, our residential projects in New York are different to our residential projects in Sydney.

Are there instances where Design Technology may obstruct rather than support great design?

SB: Technology can be a barrier when the results you can achieve are too seductive. This seductiveness can be geometry exploration, to false-colour diagrams of analysis which may not mean anything, to beautiful looking visualisations. Some of the more seductive, yet cliché aspects of parametric design can be so easy to do that they hamper wider design exploration.

How do you prepare yourself for what the future will bring in terms of Technology advance?

SB: Where I see us going as an industry (and as a firm) is to move out of a platform-centric approach towards an ecosystem of tools with services becoming available as micro-components of larger modules. We, as a company, can design our own workflow and effectively assemble our own delivery kit. It might use a lot of the Autodesk kit; it might not and instead use our own custom kit that gets thrown in there for certain parts. Maybe our own visualisation engine, maybe we pick the Epic Games' Unreal engine for the viewports, but we may combine it with little bits from Autodesk for the back end.

I imagine that in the first stage, Revit will remain the primary delivery and authoring tool, but we are going to add all sorts of other functions, such as analysis engines and visualisation tools. We are seeing the first signs of this new ecosystem with tools like Rhino. Inside Revit. Woods Bagot now has a Speckle server, and we work with its developer (and others) to advance the tool. We are dealing with software interoperability conversations centred around dataflow. We own our own cloud engines, we build our own connectors, and we develop data schemas. Whether it is a large-scale comprehensive approach or just simply a focus on energy analysis, it is all about curating the information flow and a modular approach to the design process and corresponding design tools.

3.3 More Flexible/Smaller/Lighter

Next to their increasing benefits as decision-support environments, the need for lightweight, flexible, and easy-access applications has been a major discussion point among Design Technology experts. 'Access' in this context is not limited to the notion of 'purchase-options' for software but to lowering the adoption thresholds associated to their implementation by architecture firms. How well do these tools fit with the workflow of a practice? How easily can their use be disseminated? How quickly can they be swapped for something more fitting (once required)? Licensing options and the overall business model for the dissemination of design software keep changing. Until recently, large design software providers (such as Adobe or Autodesk) were bundling their tools into dedicated 'all-rounder' suites with multiple in-house applications. Design firms could easily find themselves getting locked into purchasing those suites and end up paying big money while using only a portion of what they subscribed to. Towards the end of the 2010s, software providers increasingly realised that users want more flexibility in their software management and the associated licensing. Instead of buying a piece of software and installing it from a disk (as was commonly practiced by architecture firms since the 1990s), more and more providers now offer subscription models where users download software online and pay only for the duration of utilisation. In doing so, practices are moving away from 'owning software' to acquiring temporary licenses for its use.

The price point of the subscription typically prioritises longer-terms application over short (e.g., monthly) subscription to tools. Yet overall, the subscription option becomes attractive to practices with unpredictable workloads and associated software needs, but it also allows firms to pick and choose which applications allow them to be most productive at any point in time.

Software developers typically offer a core application that can be expanded via their own or third-party plug-ins. They protect the APIs of their application and remain mostly in control of hosting these plug-ins (in particular those of commercial value) via their app stores.[19] In contrast software developers such as McNeel opted to protect only the API of their core modelling tool Rhino, whilst allowing and promoting their user-base to create and distribute custom plug-ins. The majority of these are freely available, resulting in a lively and vivid community of users who extend Rhino's capability with hundreds of different applications. Here, users are encouraged to advance the functionality of plug-ins via peer-to-peer support, direct feedback to those developing applications, and debugging of any issues via online discussion forums. Users have a greater choice for selecting the type of plug-in that suits their needs best and customise (and add to) it in order to give it the best fit with their desired design process.

A lively user base has emerged around McNeel's Rhino and the associated Grasshopper plug-in. Grasshopper in particular sees widespread proliferation due to the broad availability of Rhino as a modelling tool and the mostly open-source, easy access of associated apps that expand its capabilities. The underlying project geometry can be associated with building performance parameters, geometry rationalisation scripts, generative design solvers, or pretty much any other design constraints that can be quantified. McNeel not only makes it easy for their core platform Rhino/Grasshopper to be expanded

---

19 Available at: https://apps.autodesk.com/en (Accessed: 31 October 2022). Also at: https://exchange.adobe.com/creativecloud.html (Accessed: 31 October 2022).

by others, but they also proactively support developers and users via the food4Rhino online portal. There, a broader community of users share their experience, learn about dedicated software training, provide feedback on any glitches in the countless auxiliary applications, and access a great number of free and paid plug-ins.

The Rhino/Grasshopper plug-ins get easily installed and experience widespread use in practice. Examples include the environmental analysis tools Ladybug/Honeybee, the live physics engine Kangaroo, the generative solver Galapagos, or the multifunctional panelling/shape generator tool Lunchbox (to name just a few). The major advantage of the Rhino/Grasshopper family of tools and plug-ins is the users' ability to combine or move across different types of investigation based on the same parametrically defined geometric model. Design morphology, performance, and other criteria can be explored using different constraints and different options without the need to remodel each time a new iteration gets examined. Depending on in-house capability, design firms use these applications on their own to test (e.g.) façade panelisation options, or they expand them via expert scripting in languages such as Python.

The next step away from heavyweight desktop applications towards more flexible use of generative design is exemplified by a service such as Hypar™. Here, the business model extends on the automation routines described earlier with TestFit. Users do not have to install an application onto their machines. Instead, they take advantage of a pre-configured, cloud-based knowledge warehouse, where they can mix and match generative design strategies to come up with novel design concepts. Hypar thereby assists designers to generate and evaluate multiple options of their design via a web interface. The environment draws on existing building data and open-source element libraries to run through different optimisation routines. In the same vein as Hypar but offering a broad scale of simulation applications (that are not necessarily limited to architectural design) is the online platform HASH™. HASH[20] is a cloud-based system for creating, visualising, and exploring simulations out of 'composable parts', built around a community of users who share their simulations and components. The key attraction of the simulations offered via HASH is the speed at which results can be achieved (without the need for software install or complicated licensing models). Another application framework worth mentioning is the online simulation platform SimScale™ that offers users a service to run so-called Computational Fluid Dynamics or other simulations involving 'Finite Element Analysis' in the cloud. SimScale uses span from product design to the optimisation of heat transfer in mechanical systems, all the way to testing windspeed/pressures on and around buildings in larger urban settings. As much as some of its use for architectural design is as yet to be confirmed, Hypar, MASH™, and SimScale, all shine a light on where software development (and not just in the architectural space) is headed: away from heavy all-rounder applications that require local installation on servers or desktop machines, toward more flexible (and potentially open access) applications that sit in the cloud, get accessed via web interfaces, and are applied for highly specific targets. Interoperability and connectivity between data from different applications thereby becomes pivotal.

Design Technology leadership will be increasingly required to monitor and manage the integration of cloud-based tools/services into a firm's workflow. It promises greater flexibility to their staff, who will be less reliant on a specific tool (and associated licensing). At the same time, it will become more difficult to

---

20 Available at: https://hash.ai/ (Accessed: 31 October 2022).

provide support and training if staff can pick and choose whatever tool they see as the best fit for resolving a specific problem. When it comes to the inclusion of automation routines, question should be asked about the value proposition of targeted algorithms to help repetitive tasks, while minimising the time/effort to write/access the underlying algorithms. Hence, rather than looking at ways a firm would typically address these issues and coming up with smart support infrastructures that tie into these processes, DT ties in perfectly with the design culture of that organisation.

If one uses predefined algorithms, one might end up with same-ness of responses. This is probably acceptable for simple, repetitive tasks where resolving complexity is the issue but not necessarily providing the kind of 'conversation with the designer' that architectural designers want.

3.4   The Virtual Office

Most of this chapter has so far tackled design tools and associated ecologies, yet another aspect of Design Technology has seen a dramatic increase in uptake since the early 2020s: enabling remote working and interactive/immersive engagement with virtual models.

Remote working is not new to design practice. For years, many larger firms (or those collaborating with others in geographically disperse locations) have relied on teleconferencing and sharing of documentation via cloud-based systems. Yet, typically, interaction about key design decisions would still occur predominantly via face-to-face meetings, frequently supported via pin-up/markup sessions and the use of physical work-in-progress models. If remote working was rather the exception in design practice before early 2020, it became the de facto standard overnight, once most advanced economies globally had to stop or drastically reduce office-based operations due to COVID-19 restrictions. Suddenly, Design Technology teams (joined by IT) were in the spotlight, offering staff a lifeline by rapidly setting up remote working IT and DT infrastructures to allow them to work from home. Next, they needed to establish collaboration processes to align with the different workflow intrinsic to a home office setting. Those who already used a cloud-based design modelling system had an easier transition to documenting from home, yet designers still had to get used to replacing face-to-face design meetings and document markups with a virtual office setting online.

In retrospect, one could speculate that many design firms 'got away with murder'; if the pandemic had hit five to seven years earlier, they would likely have experienced major productivity losses or even ground to a halt due to inadequate software and network infrastructures. In the years before the start of the pandemic, many of the tools that got them through the turbulent times did not even exist, or they had only just hit the market. As an example, the teleconferencing tool Zoom™ (which alongside Microsoft TEAMs™ counts towards the most common applications for office staff to interface remotely) only integrated functionality for 'multiple screen and device meetings in HD' in mid-2017.[21] Similarly, online whiteboarding/graphic collaboration tools like Miro, Mural™, Lucidspark™, or Milanote™ only became available to a mass market shortly before or during the pandemic.

---

21 Dignan, L. (2017) 'Polycom, Zoom Forge Video Conferencing, Collaboration Pact', *ZDNet*. Available at: www.zdnet.com/article/polycom-zoom-forge-video-conferencing-collaboration-pact/ (Accessed: 31 October 2022).

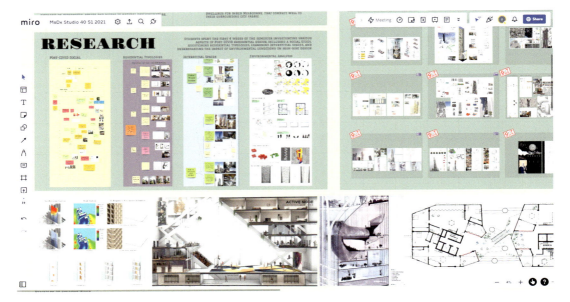

▲ Figure 3.10

Example of a Miro Board for digital annotation, sketches, and team information exchange.
© Dominik Holzer

These tools have proven essential to assist architecture firms to share highly visible content online and (in most cases) allow for team markups and annotations, comment posting, and other graphically based collaboration activities. Even with face-to-face collaboration becoming more common again, all signs point towards a sustained use of online whiteboarding tools for design practices that operate and manage/log their conversations about design progress on projects. Next to establishing a seamless transition from office to remote working for design and documentation activities, Design Technology teams were frequently confronted with a different challenge: at the outset of the pandemic, designers who heavily relied on physical prototyping as part of their workflow lost access to model workshops and FabLabs and therefore access to their physical models for design exploration.

Restricted access to physical models disrupted the workflow within firms who normally rely on such artefacts in their ideation process. Making a virtue of necessity, Design Technology teams now investigate opportunities of Virtual Reality to help compensate for the reduced access to physical models (whilst offering other features as well), and they introduce Augmented Reality to expand on their capability for interfacing actual and virtual models as part of their design process.

If the previously high cost of setup and equipment, plus the need for dedicated spaces for its installation, had prevented most architecture firms to engage with VR as part of everyday practice, VR technology has become far more accessible from the early 2010s. Portable headsets such as the Oculus Rift (or similar) introduced VR-use to a mass market.[22] At that time, the gaming industry made major advances in developing easy-access first-user 3D visualisation (both software and hardware), and their knowledge was quickly transferred to the

---

22 Carreiro, M. and Pinto, P. (2013) 'The Evolution of Representation in Architecture', *Future Traditions [1st eCAADe Regional International Workshop Proceedings/*ISBN 978–989–8527–03–5], University of Porto, Faculty of Architecture, Portugal, 4–5 April 2013, pp. 27–38.

building industry. Three-dimensional game engines like Unity3D and Unreal can import lightweight virtual architectural models as 3D backdrop for VR/AR, with direct interfaces now available to ready BIM files for such systems on the fly.[23] Still, pre-pandemic, VR and AR were rather seen as a 'niche' aspect of Design Technology with limited immediate applicability in a design context. This has now clearly changed with COVID, as a great number of leading firms had limited access to physical models, and hence now use VR/AR to enrich their design and delivery workflows.

As part of this more widespread proliferation of VR and AR, the technology now gets increasingly used early in the design process to assist in form finding or other formative ideation processes. Simultaneously, AR in particular sees increased adoption when interfacing design models with real-life contexts (e.g., during site visit). AR allows designers to juxtapose and overlay actual site-specific context to virtual models to verify the adequacy of solutions to be implemented. Additionally, AR gets used to assist construction teams to assess health and safety risks on site or to assist with assembly/construction processes via animated features.

One firm that has heavily invested in their VR and AR capabilities over the past few years is the Basel-based Herzog & de Meuron. Traditionally using physical model making extensively as part of their design ideation, their recent embrace of VR and AR opens unprecedented opportunities to the firm.

---

23 Alizadehsalehi, S., Hadavi, A. and Huang, J.C. (2020) 'From BIM to Extended Reality in AEC Industry', *Automation in Construction*, 116, p. 103254.

▼ **Figure 3.11**

Design team using VR during
design review meeting.
© Herzog & de Meuron

HERZOG & DE MEURON

The design ideation at Herzog & de Meuron is a highly structured, well informed process, hand in hand with input from Jaques and Pierre at critical points of a design progression. A fundamental element of this approach is the use of physical models to inform various aspects of a project, from early morphology, tectonic logic, articulation of spaces, all the way to material definitions, and one-to-one-scale mock-ups of componentry to be installed. A project's design ontology can be traced via those models, hand in hand with the referring sketches and drawings; for that reason, models get meticulously catalogued and stored at a dedicated facility (the Kabinett). In times of digital practice and virtual models, Design Technology starts to play an increasingly pivotal role in informing and augmenting this approach. In the recent past, the practice has actively been exploring BIM and VR/AR as additional tools in their arsenal. Steffen Riegas and Michael Drobnik spearhead the firm's Digital Practice (and as part of that, also their Design Technology) team. Here they discuss how their work is currently positioned within the practice and where it is headed.

What role does Design Technology play at Herzog & de Meuron? How do you implement it to support the firm's distinctive approach?

Michael Drobnik (MD): The practice's design approach is the key driver to what we do. The DT Team provides suitable digital methods and procedures to support the resolution of questions that stem from the design process. In this sense, Design Technology clearly plays a supporting, not a leading role.

Steffen Riegas (SR): But we also like to try out new things and explore unchartered territory because we want to innovate and evolve. Doing so, we sometimes must accept calculated risks and allow ourselves to test all kinds of new things and processes. We have multiple roles. On one hand, we are clearly a support organ and make sure everything runs smoothly; on the other hand, It is our role to be disruptive.

▼ Figure 3.12

AR Experiments, example 1: design morphology.
© Herzog & de Meuron

PRACTICE INSERT: Herzog & de Meuron

How is Design Technology integrated at Herzog & de Meuron on an organisational level?

SR: The Design Technologies Group operates with about twenty staff. Although we have experts in BIM, scripting, modelling, visualisation, VR/AR, or for our digital model making workshop, our concept is to combine this diversity under one roof together. Many on our team have multiple overlapping fields of expertise. At one point, we considered a potential split into two separate groups, since the BIM team was growing rapidly, but we decided against it.

Organisationally we act like a horizontal ribbon that connects all projects with specific interfaces at certain points. To reach out to the project teams, we established and foster specialists groups across the office, which bring team members from different projects and our DT specialists together. For instance, the responsible architects for the BIM processes on each project.

▲ Figure 3.13

AR Hololens application on the Kinderspital (Zürich) construction site.
© Herzog & de Meuron

Which management structures do you have in place to effectively apply Design Technology at Herzog & de Meuron?

SR: The group grew constantly over the years. At its core it was focusing on topics that arose from managing software applications that became more and more relevant tools for architects. In the 1990s those were mainly the CAD applications. Especially the emergence of 3D modelling unfolded new digital disciplines like visualisation or manufacturing. Already back then, we always embraced those new possibilities and tried to make them part of our work. Following this principle, we equipped the model-making workshop with CNC machines or built-up extensive know-how around rendering and CGI in general. At first the group was named 'CAD-CAM' group and gathered a few individuals with that kind of profile. With the digital landscape becoming more and more divers, we "rebranded" to Design Technologies Group, or simply DT, some years later. This changed a lot in regard to the overall awareness of the significance of the group to the design process.

▲ Figure 3.14

Stadtcasino (Basel), construction detail of railing, archival reference, and CNC milling technology.
© Herzog & de Meuron

Are there any cultural clashes between Designers and Technology/Technologists at Herzog & de Meuron?

SR: Almost everyone in the DT group has a background as architect and hence has the right sensitivity to engage with the project teams and their issues. As architects, we always work in multidisciplinary teams, where individuals with many different talents and interests come together and collaborate. In the end we provide informed input, but it is up to the project lead to decide which process the team should adopt; we support them whichever path they want to take.

▶ Figure 3.15

Design Technologies group presentation.
© Herzog & de Meuron

▶ Figure 3.16

3D scanned digitally posed models, digital rendering, light and material study.
© Herzog & de Meuron

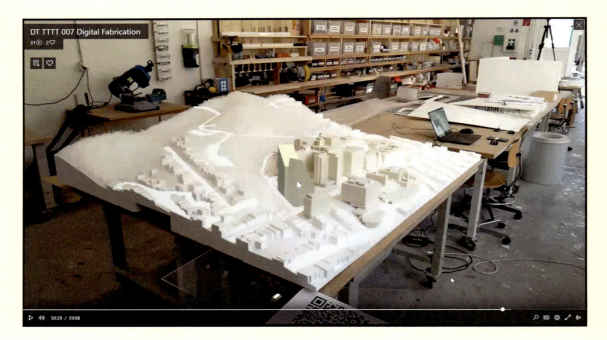

▲ Figure 3.17

AR Experiments, example 2: physical context model augmentation.
© Herzog & de Meuron

MD: The most accurate image for a DT person is that of the T-shaped skill set. Especially when it comes to process-focused support, the Senior BIM Managers quickly become part of the project's management and leadership team. We provide our expertise, advise on workflows, and check on deliverables. In addition, we are aware of any other relevant processes that overlap or even conflict with our tasks or role.

Do you then embed that staff member in the project team, or does the Digital Technology group operate remotely from a centralised area?

SR: We are physically located in the centre of the practice. Our colleagues can simply walk up to our desks or post their questions in a group chat to get support with software. We can provide support for 3D modelling applications, parametric design, or scripting without being full members of the project team. We usually work with the teams on very specific topics, so most of our hours can be billed directly to the respective projects. It is important that the Design Technology team is not seen as a black box, where we all do research in isolation and are disconnected from the reality of the projects and then unexpectedly emerge with a solution a few weeks later (that maybe no one needs).

MD: Adopting BIM is a still ongoing transformation process and colleagues require extensive support, and therefore co-location with members of a project team is desirable. There is a fair chance that our BIM managers become tied into the project team and accompany them throughout a project phase.

At Herzog & de Meuron, are there any instances where new technology can introduce to your Partners solutions that they may not have considered otherwise?

SR: Sure, there is a general open-minded atmosphere towards new ideas, technologies, and ultimately the design outcomes in the practice. The focus usually lies on a potential new architectural quality independently of whether or not it was utilising new technologies. For example, constantly emerging new methods help us make building components. Naturally, we are very interested in exploring these, especially if they enable us to produce objects or artefacts that expand our repertoire. Take CNC milling: it is not just that using a technology automates manufacturing processes, making them faster or more precise. Each process leaves its mark on the finished objects, and we may be intrigued by the structures or patterns with which certain routing algorithms have shaped the objects.

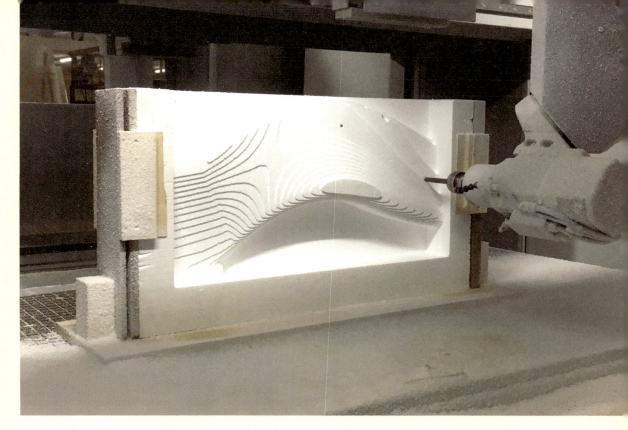

▲ Figure 3.18

Robotic CNC milled 1:1 prototype of handrail detail, PS foam.
© Herzog & de Meuron

Do you have a typical workflow when it comes to interfacing sketching with digital design exploitation tools such as Rhino and then with documentation tools in BIM?

MD: In early design stages, there will always be disruptions to the flow of information; it is not a linear process with seamless interfaces from one tool to another. As much as presenting design tasks with clarity and precision is pivotal in the design meetings with our partners, one has to find the best possible way to get information across. This often means breaking the digital workflow and introducing more manual processes for post-production and the fine-tuning of content. It is essential for us to understand the highly agile design process in order to be able to support it in an optimal way via digital tool ecologies but also understand when to step away from them in order to get the best results.

▶ Figure 3.19

Kinderspital (Children's Hospital Zürich) – shaded/rendered section through detailed BIM.
© Herzog & de Meuron

PRACTICE INSERT: Herzog & de Meuron

125

SR: Looking at the tools we use, Rhino is an extremely interesting and useful tool for us. Virtually everyone on a design team is familiar with Rhino. It should be as natural as sketching with a pencil. We can use Rhino to create schematic models at the beginning of the design process, quickly create 3D geometry, and visualise it via rendered output. It also allows us to quickly capture volumetric and surface information. We often then leave the Rhino/GH context and transfer the information into BIM tools for documentation. As we get closer to construction, Rhino comes back into play to help us with complex design details or to go directly into manufacturing processes.

MD: We are constantly evolving the way we connect BIM tools and other applications such as Rhino. Currently we are following two approaches. One is to find a smart way to build connections between different platforms. Rhino. Inside as part of Rhino7 seems to be a promising way forward. The other approach is to transfer a BIM methodology and designing with information into earlier design stages but without using a full documentation-oriented BIM platform. Basically, the idea is to work with a few attributes associated with geometry and give it the ability to colour, calculate, and export information to CSV or PowerBI. We call that approach BIM light.

Are you comparing notes with your satellite offices, and how do you collaborate with them when it comes to advancing and applying Design Technology?

MD: Traditionally we are very much centralised in Basel, all partners of the firm are here; all workshops (plus the Kabinett – our physical model collection which we use as a learning tool to inform design processes across projects) are located here as well. We call our central facilities in Basel the Campus, and in fact it works and feels quite like a university walking through the studios at busy times. But things have changed not only due to the pandemic. For DT it even means that we have now started expanding permanently to our satellite offices. We have largely and quickly moved to collaboration tools, which means we can now work more closely with our satellites. The Tech Talks which used to take place in the largest meeting rooms we now broadcast live on our intranet.

▼ Figure 3.20

The Kabinett, virtual/physical model AR overlay.
© Herzog & de Meuron

What are the limitations of Design Technology use at Herzog & de Meuron?

MD: Limitations do exist. For the Serpentine Gallery Pavilion one of the early study models was made of candle wax. Rhino, Revit, or any other digital tool would have been a wrong choice at this early concept stage. A pencil sketch or clay model often offers a fairly good conceptual description of an idea. Even at later design stages, such tools can be useful to work out specific details in a more focused manner. We mentioned earlier that we might go from Rhino to Revit and back to Rhino on some projects; I would like to add that we, of course, also go back to tracing-paper and pencil before going back to the computer. Architects still have to work things out on site, and a project architect may discuss a detail with a builder by sketching straight on a concrete wall.

How does Design Technology at H&deM evolve over time?

SR: Since we do not know what the future brings, we can try to shape it. For us It is important to take part in the development of the digital tools we are using. We have long maintained close relationships with the companies and people who create the tools. Our feedback on the products and discussing our individual challenges with them have a positive impact for all of us. In parallel we keep a lively exchange with our peers from other firms. There are countless opportunities at councils, conferences, or universities to meet and exchange ideas. And at last digital innovation does not respond well to a top-down business case. It is based on a bottom-up approach of how we can best support our design teams.

3.5 File to Fabrication

Among leading architecture firms, it has become increasingly common to use Design Technology to inform the fabrication of bespoke building components. The most obvious example of this approach is the definition of highly bespoke façade solutions, as well as structural systems including secondary steel or cross-laminated (or smart) timber elements. In recent years, several architecture firms have specialised in developing customs solutions for building components jointly with local fabricators, or in some instances, via in-depth inhouse prototyping. In most instances, these approaches are supported via bespoke Design Technology setups that allow for material testing and the interface between 3D models and fabrication equipment. Virtual models are thereby not simply detailed for geometrical representation (or BIM-type documentation), but they are geared towards what can be fabricated and assembled with as little effort as possible and the support of automated CAD/CAM (computer aided design/computer aided manufacture) interfaces. As a side effect, these file-to-manufacture approaches challenge existing supply chains and reduce the need for 2D documentation in some cases. Most recently, the use of robotic assembly offers designers even more freedom to explore/create complex building components and systems.

The opportunities inherent to Design Technology allowing architects to reclaim (parts of) their previous role as 'makers' have been well documented in the literature.[24,25] On a project level, they unfold by deeper investigation into material behaviour, and digital production processes. Leading design firms foster close collaboration between their design and fabrication equipment specialist contractors and fabricators who are willing and able to take on the challenge of producing bespoke, non-standard building components. This interface does not happen overnight. For this kind of collaboration to be successful, both parties need to adjust their work processes and find common ground for information transfer and fabrication procedures.[26,27] Architects on one hand need to be aware, at least in general terms, of the fabrication constraints presented by the fabricators' machinery. They also need to be able to describe the underlying geometry of their desired bespoke solutions in great detail, allowing them to break down and subdivide their topographical models into discrete elements for fabrication. Next to that process, an open dialogue between the designer and the fabricator is essential to determine the exact (data) interfaces between the geometry and the fabrication models. Interviews with leading practices revealed an entire spectrum of possible solutions on how this interface gets manifested. On the other hand, architects may use manufacturing-level software such as Solidworks™, CATIA, or specific plug-ins for Rhino, that allow them to include material properties and fabrication constraints into their models. On the other end of the spectrum, architects rely on the skill of the manufacturers to translate their surface models into buildable entities. How the fabrication process ultimately unfolds depends on market capability of manufacturers (local or geographically disperse), their pre-existing skill level, the designer's familiarity with the fabricator's equipment, and the desired level of control exerted by the architects. A third and frequently applied option is for the architects to work with third-party specialists who take over the role of bridging from design to fabrication,

---

24 Sheil, B. (ed.) (2005) 'Design Through Making', *AD Architectural Design*, Vol. 75. No. 4.
25 Kolarevic, B. and Klinger, K. (2008) *Manufacturing Material Effects: Rethinking Design and Making in Architecture*, Routledge, London.
26 Dunn, N. (2012) *Digital Fabrication in Architecture*, Laurence King Publishing, London.
27 Yuan, P.F., Leach, N. and Menges, A. (2018) *Digital Fabrication*, Tongji University Press, Shanghai.

thereby ensuring the architect's interest are represented while maximising the automation capability of the fabricators.

The project architect will be a driving force to help determine how model data is appropriated towards the fabrication effort. In many instances, the design and documentation process might start in surface modelling tools, to then move into object-oriented BIM tools for documentation, for bespoke elements to move back again into the surface-modelling software to facilitate the fabrication process. The Design Technology experts on the project ensure that the 3D models used as a template (or even as a blueprint) for fabrication are accurate. In some instances, this will require coding of bespoke solutions to interface between geometric properties and fabrication-related instructions for the manufacturing equipment. The use of multi-axis arm manipulator robots is providing an ever growing array of opportunities to designers in translating complex solutions into buildable componentry. In some instances, Design Technology experts assist in the development of the robots' end-effectors in pursuit of a bespoke fabrication solution.

▲ Figure 3.21

Power to Make (Melbourne), fabrication workshop setup.
© Power to Make + LLDS

One theme resonates strongly with leading design firms is the desire to cut out the 'middle-man' when it comes to moving from design to the creation of building components. To achieve this, Design Technology becomes an enabler that facilitates direct translation of bespoke geometrical articulation (such as manifested in a façade panel system) into buildable components that are code-compliant and that can be assembled locally at the construction site by a team of enabled contractors. The ability to control geometry to such a level of detail has long been removed from architects, who often saw their ideas being 'value-engineered' out as manufacturing skills/abilities of local contractors would have been prohibitive or the fabrication process simply too costly to allow the translation from computer model to the built artefact.

In order to understand how leading design firms overcome this issue via Design Technology, one first needs to consider the supply chains they typically interact with in their translation from design to built artefact. Most parts of the 20th century were marked by what is typically referred to Industry 2.0 and 3.0 manufacturing processes: mass production, automated assembly, and the beginning of the information age via the use of computers and associated networks.[28] Key to achieving decent productivity levels for construction was the reliance on globally standardised building components that allowed fabricators to use a predetermined set of fabrication equipment to mass-produce high quantities at a low price and high levels of quality assurance. In that regard, most fabrication equipment up to the start of the third millennium was highly inflexible and not geared up for producing non-standard structural systems or cladding/panelisation options. This restrictive manufacturing characteristic stood in strong contrast to the expanding abilities of designers to generate daring geometrical concepts via 3D software. Those who dared to build them would likely risk budget blowouts or getting into disputes with their contractors who would not know how to translate what looked good on screen into (e.g.) an actual façade system.

Increased automation and networked communication between cyber and physical systems inherent to Industry 4.0 Digitisation, bring custom fabrication of building components within the reach of architects.[29] This also means that globalisation is playing a major role in enabling architecture firms to identify collaborators on a global market, whose machinery and fabrication processes match their design aspirations. A great example of the rapid changes to the architect–fabricator interaction can be seen when comparing Coop Himmelb(l)au's Musée des Confluences in Lyon (France) with their work on the Museum of Contemporary Art & Planning Exhibition (MOCAPE) in Shenzhen (China).

◀ Figure 3.22

Pick and place robotic research mock-up.
© Coop Himmelb(l)au

---

28 Review: Identification of roadmap of fourth construction industrial revolution, Sen, Lau et al. (2019) 'IOP Conference Series: Materials Science and Engineering, Volume 615', *7th International Conference on Euro Asia Civil Engineering Forum 30 September to 2 October 2019*, Stuttgart, Germany.

29 Zakoldaev, D.A. et al. (2020) 'Industry 4.0 vs Industry 3.0: The Role of Personnel in Production', *IOP Conference Series: Materials Science and Engineering*, Vol. 734, II International Scientific Conference, "Advanced Technologies in Aerospace, Mechanical and Automation Engineering" – MIST: Aerospace, November 2019, Krasnoyarsk, Russia.

Both are geometrically highly challenging and expressive, putting major emphasis on complex façade panels and associated structural systems. Construction for both projects occurred only three or four years apart, and the firm was able to leverage off their 'lessons-learned' form Lyon (where robotic fabrication and installation were not yet possible) to advance these methods on the Shenzhen project.

Many leading architects interviewed for this book aim to set up a joint workflow to allow them to interact with the fabricator's production equipment straight from their 3D files and without having to rely on 2D documentation. To facilitate this, they define fabrication constraints based on their fabricators' equipment and use geometric rationalisation techniques (with plenty of options available within the Rhino/Grasshopper software environment) to appropriate their models. The resulting geometry and associated fabrication instructions are then translated to the computer numerical construction (CNC) machinery via G-Code. CNC- enabled fabrication subsequently occurs with precisely controlled routers and/or cutters that can work with 3D objects depending on the amount of axis of movement required for their toolpath (defining the coordinate locations that the equipment will follow for the machining process).

▼ Figure 3.23

Swatch building, prefabrication of structural timber-shell members.
© Design-to-Production

The CNC process is different from the use of Robotic equipment. Robotic arm manipulators are not addressed via G-code, but they have a higher interface software language associated to them. At this point, there is no standard process applied across the industry, but there are multiple possible workflows. The principle remains the same: users generate a motion path with the typical CAD applications available to them; the programming tool subsequently generates the robotic execution program based on that CAD definition.[30] As one brand of

---

30 Available at: https://pdfs.semanticscholar.org/688f/3e2b829bbbde40b0e8a165a7 10f003127935.pdf (Accessed: 31 October 2022).

robots' processes information differently from another brand, operators tend to use a mix of applications that reinterpret these movement paths to produce commands for robot motion (e.g., FabUnion), which then interface with the bespoke software of the robot's manufacturer (e.g., RobotStudio™ for ABB or Kuka PRC).

In most instances, architecture firms work closely with local specialist fabricators who take over this part of the fabrication process. Paul Loh, co-owner of the Melbourne-based micro-manufacturing facility Power to Make[31] has assisted a number of world-leading architects in realising their ideas and reflects on his interface with these firms: 'The more knowledgeable practices tend to align with our software workflow, i.e. they provide Rhino Model/Grasshopper definition or compatible file type (such as IGS, STEP). Very rarely do architects prepare the cut file as they never get the protocol correct'.

One example of a successful collaboration can be seen on DS+R Shed in NYC. The project architect advanced his geometry definition in a CATIA file (consisting predominantly of non-standard steel profiles) in an interactive process, based on feedback from the steel shop fabricators. Together they created the blueprint for the fabricator's production machinery to cut out and bend individual steel plates in an automated and cost-effective way. It was a highly symbiotic relationship that rewrote how both parties approach the design and realisation of non-standard geometry. A workflow that envisages moving straight from complex 3D models to fabrication also needs to involve engineers who share the same level of flexibility with their analysis and simulation tools as the others, to warrant code compliance and (structural/environmental/fire) integrity bespoke components.

The final practice-section of this book (LASSA) highlights how boutique design firms can adopt an approach to fabrication that leads to entire new business models for marketing/promoting/expanding their presence in certain markets.

---

31 Available at: https://powertomake.com.au/ (Accessed: 31 October 2022).

▼ Figure 3.24
KHI House – under construction, aerial view.
© LASSA

PRACTICE INSERT: LASSA

LASSA is one of those smaller, agile firms that consciously apply Design Technology to manifest their distinctive design approach. The studio benefits from continued cross-fertilisation between academia and practice (founders Dora Sweijd and Theo Lalos teach at London's AA), with projects spanning from Europe to the Middle East and Asia. LASSA question the role of the architect as maker, highly conscious of the socio-economic context of their projects. As Theo Sarantoglou Lalis explains, LASSA apply innovative ways to work with constraint budgets to get involved in fabrication processes both hands-on and via digital means.

As a small-scale, boutique design firm, how do you use technology to your advantage in a competitive market?

Theo Lalis (TL): When we started the office in 2009, the geopolitical context demanded from us to think more carefully about social implications and economy. Dora and I made the very deliberate decision to work towards the democratisation of non-standard form, by thinking of ways of implementing our experience with large-scale digital fabrication in the previous decade on mundane commissions. How can that way of working and that way of thinking about architectural production be deployed on simple commissions with regular budgets? Our position was to explore where that digital culture is viable, where it is interesting, and where it can bring progress. These were the beginnings. As the practice grew, we decided to invest in our own prototyping lab.

◀ Figures 3.25

Villa Ypsilon, material and assembly prototyping for lost formwork/6 mm ply formwork surface with ribbing.
© LASSA

When we built the Villa Ypsilon in Greece, we were dealing with a double curved concrete shell to be constructed in a remote area. Obviously, the local contractors did not have the know-how to realise it. As part of self-funded research, we decided to move into a bigger warehouse space and bought a CNC machine. We prototyped the formwork, manufactured it in Brussels, shipped it, and assembled it in four days. That way we were able to work with local contractors and benefit from local construction costs, because all the complexity was managed through the remote prefabrication of moulds and formwork. We were able to do in-house structural and environmental analysis, the automation, and the manufacturing of the formwork.

Our ability to do this as a small firm has to do with the software maturity that allowed us to engage with processes, which would traditionally have been the work of specialist consultants.

▲ Figure 3.26
Villa Ypsilon, exterior view of finished project.
© LASSA

What role does Design Technology play at LASSA?

TL: It enables us to work in locations with low skills and low budgets, and nevertheless achieve a level of complexity. We have developed an interest in form integration. We see form in the practice as an accumulation of constraints. We then use Design Technology to integrate into one form multiple design objectives such as structure, circulation, environmental performance, acoustics, and constraints related to construction processes. It became part of our design approach. We have a clear commitment to making things affordable and to taking economy and the logistics of fabrication very seriously. As an example, on a tower project, we managed to work with our native method, meaning to work in 3D directly, to automate the production of drawings through various bridges and scripting between programs. It enabled us to respond to very fast-paced demands from the client with a very small team. Responding to changes to 600 A0 plans in less than a week, without the need of having 15 people working on the job. We had a budget for a standard, rectangular tower, and because we were able to interface with industry, we could afford a level of customisation of the façade. Our interest in the transfer of technology enabled us to find bespoke constructive solutions outside the construction industry and to speak with manufacturers directly.

▼ Figure 3.27
Villa Ypsilon: (a) formwork/site assembly of ribbing for double curved formwork. © LASSA; (b) living room view, double curved lost formwork with acoustic ribbing and light integration. © naaro.

▲ Figure 3.27
(Continued)

▲ Figure 3.28

KHI House – aerial view.
© naaro

How do you integrate Design Technology on an organisational level? Do you have specialists dedicated to different aspects of design?

TL: Personally, I do not believe in specialisation; people do not flourish professionally in this way. Our staff are trained and are able to do various things. We do not have a rendering person, we do not have a production design person, everybody can do wind-simulation and structural analysis as well as all other essential design tasks.

Which management structures do you have in place to efficiently apply Design Technology?

TL: We have two partners and other staff, but numbers are fluctuating. We use our connection with academia to test certain things. More recently, we experimented with AR on physical models – 3D-scanning those models, integrating them into gaming engines, and things like that. It is not the typical workflow most design practices would engage in. We may organise an academic workshop, where we bring in a specialist from Microsoft, and then try to develop with him/her a bespoke workflow that fits in with our design ethos and working methods. We then transfer that knowledge back to the office. My project leaders very much embrace this approach.

▶ Figure 3.29
KHI House, expanded polystyrene formwork: (a) aerial view and (b) detail.
© LASSA

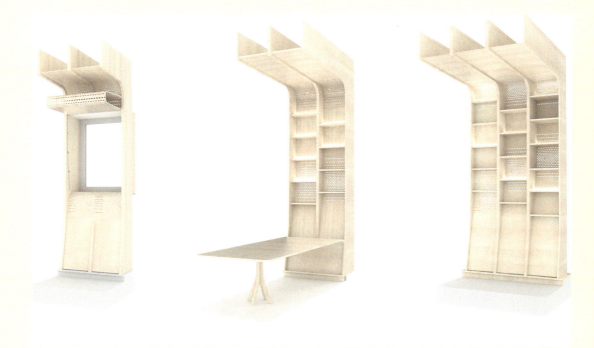

▲ Figure 3.30

Pocket Nursery, three modules digital model.
© LASSA

Do you ever use delivery tools (because you might have to) such as Revit? Do you ever use these more back-end documentation tools?

TL: Revit is quite powerful in drawing generation but not very interesting as a design tool. For the tower project, because of the many variables (such as louvers or glazing types), we designed everything in Grasshopper, and in Rhino. Via links that did not exist at the time with Revit [in 2012], we developed a custom connection that enabled us to automate the drawing process. We spent a lot of time implementing our layer system, but then drawing-generation was fast. We have tried using CATIA but have found it very stiff. It is very powerful in interfacing with manufacturers directly from our 3D files, but it does not work that well for drawing generation.

The interesting thing about the house in Greece is that it was practically executed via paperless construction. In order for our millimetre-accurate formwork to fit, we had to involve the builder. We did easy supervision, and the drawings just had a legal purpose. Drawing today is in a bit of a crisis. It remains a necessity, as its output represents a legal document, but the drawings are not necessarily important for the construction in certain cases. At the same time, the drawing's role as a cultural agent is revived.

Are there any cultural clashes between design and technology at LASSA?

TL: I can tell you one example. Half the office is working on a master plan in China; the other half produces guides for a small-scale residential project we design. The guys that did the guides were frustrated, they wanted to do conception. At the time, they did not realise that what they were working on was much more meaningful and novel than another schematic design package. That happened at some point, especially amongst younger staff, who wanted to work on competitions.

Are there instances at LASSA where you struggle to identify which software pathway is preferable?

TL: We are not committed to any particular package or way of working. Our skill comes from our ability and interest to design new workflows, depending on software opportunity. Software evolves very fast these days, together with computing power. 'New tools' also means risk. We deal with risk via our capacity to prototype things.

What would be a typical example of how you bring R&D from academia into your projects?

TL: With the commissions we have, there exist latent ideas that we are exploring with students, and we are looking for opportunities to implement them. If that implies acquiring external knowledge or buying a Kuka robot on a six-meter rail, we will do it. We 'design' commissions in such a way, that they become opportunities to test things or to bring ideas to maturity. We look for projects that are basically sponsoring research. Our ability to take risk at the smaller scale is greater than on a very large corporate project

How do you work across your different office locations.

TL: LASSA is registered in London, but because the lack of space, we decided to locate the Fab Lab with the fabrication machines in Brussels; there we could accommodate it within a very large space. Initially, the bigger office was in London with fifteen people; then, as we were able to do more research, Brussels grew. It triggered new conditions and new ways of working. We still recruit staff from London, like ex-students.

▲ Figure 3.31

Pocket Nursery, modules assembly.
© LASSA

What are the limitations of Design Technology at LASSA?

TL: I wish we had a greater capability to experiment; there are certain things that I have in mind. I am just waiting for the project that will justify the expense and investment.

◀ Figure 3.32

Pocket Nursery, finished project.
© naaro

We have arrived at a stage where the technology available is sufficient for us to evolve. Overabundance of technology sometimes releases pressure on how much intelligence we put on design. We need to re-engage with design rather than be too disrupted by the robots and tools we use. There is this assumption that robotic labour is free, versus costly human labour, and if we do everything using robotics, it will be better. I do not agree with this notion. My interest right now is about the balanced use of technology, understanding how much technology is really necessary to pull it off. I have become increasingly interested in low-tech and especially the relationship between hand-labour, technology, and robotic fabrication. Working with constraints of holistic economy. . . . It is really finding the right balance of how much robotic labour we need and embedding the logistics of fabrication in the design process. If something takes six months to assemble by a robot rather than four days, it is a big problem for us in terms of the economy. How long it takes, how many tools, or how much expertise is needed is something that we integrate in the Rhino script. For example, the formwork we did, had five thousand pieces, yet no screws, no drawings, no instructional drawing, and no specialist skills required for assembly. That was a design decision. In other instances, when this is not considered, the design can take forever.

How does design Technology evolve at LASSA? Is there any research direction that you feel you would be keen on exploring?

TL: At the moment we are interested in VR, but not in the in the classical way of exporting 3D to a gaming engine. It has more to do with designing something in 3D to then manufacturing and prototyping it at another scale then we find ways of visualising or experiencing the model at that scale. We want to 3D-scan a model, to then navigate that model and subsequently overlay our design on top of that! It is about using VR as an assessment and design tool. The physical model is one stage of the design, but you can then go in there in VR and modify it. The technology is now mature enough to do that.

Other than that, we are interested in rammed earth using robotic fabrication. We currently have a commission that may justify investing in new machines. We think this construction method is extremely promising. It is the cleanest environmentally, the material is inexpensive and locally sourced, and, with the help of robotics, we can achieve formal complexity and reduce labour costs.

3.6   Convergence – Tooling Across Domains

Reflecting on how computational design tools proliferate contemporary practice, another aspect clearly stands out. In the early days of digital tools, more often than not, applications tended to focus on addressing specific goals inherent to a specific group of stakeholders. This singular focus has changed in the new millennium, with increasing emphasis given to tools that cut across professional boundaries and allow experts from various fields to evaluate, validate, and advance design options jointly (and at times concurrently) beyond their individual domains. In his 2017 publication on *Convergence*,[32] Randy Deutsch offers an in-depth overview about changes to contemporary design practice facilitated via converging fields of inquiry. Deutsch elaborates on various types of convergence, including People/People, People/Computers, Computers/Machines, and Data/Building Materials/Robotics. One of Deutsch's key observations relates to the use (and appropriation) of data in support of architectural design. The data focus goes hand in hand with the reconfiguration of processes that allow designers to access and share project data in unprecedented ways. It immediately becomes apparent that architects nowadays operate less and less in isolation, as they depend on a broad range of data inputs and outputs that tie their activities to those of their collaborators.

The increased convergence between tools needs to be facilitated on two levels: firstly, in terms of data interoperability and the connectivity of functions that can be tied to the same base geometry and, secondly, on a process-level to minimise the time lag between geometry updates and performance feedback. The more concurrent feedback can be derived, the more interactive and useful the decision support will be. Engineers or other project participants can thereby become co-authors, instead of simply re-engineering the architects' concepts. Many design firms still struggle with this approach as they still need to learn how to adjust their dialogue with their collaborators (who themselves may need to get used to their more proactive participation).

Automating Workflow Across Applications

With the ever increasing need for better management of the information content of their projects and the aim to test different scenarios with varying data inputs, design teams want to explore options and connect design parameters beyond the boundaries of bespoke applications. By the mid-2010s (open source) data platforms such as Flux or later Speckle[33] became available to assist designers to facilitate live data linkages across multiple software applications in a structured way, thereby acting as a distributed common data environment.[34] Supported by a small group of leading design firms, Flux was the first platform with wider appeal to offer a cloud-based solution to move design data across architectural, engineering, and construction domains. Less of a design software and more of an interface, Flux was hailed the 'Google Translator of the digital design world'.[35] Despite its

---

32   Deutsch, R. (2017) *Convergence – The Redesign of Design*, Wiley & Sons, Hoboken, NJ.

33   Available at: https://speckle.systems/about (Accessed: 31 October 2022).

34   Poinet, P., Stefanescu, D. and Papadonikolaki, E. (2020) 'Collaborative Workflows and Version Control Through Open-Source and Distributed Common Data Environment', *Proceedings of the 18th International Conference on Computing in Civil and Building Engineering (ICCCBE)*, São Paulo (Brazil). Available at: www.researchgate.net/publication/342419999 (Accessed: 31 October 2022).

35   Available at: www.globenewswire.com/news-release/2015/12/21/1089031/0/en/FLUX-Introduces-Collaboration-Tools-for-the-Architecture-and-Construction-Industry.html (Accessed: 31 October 2022).

noble aim and promising feedback from its dedicated users, Flux was discontinued after only five or six years of operation. This in return paved the way for Speckle to take over where Flux left off. Speckle helps users to connect between different software platforms and exchange information from different datasets whilst triggering command chains across those applications. As an open source, cloud-based platform, Speckle is expandable and can be 'hacked' by design firms to best fit their needs. The most common applications that can be connected are Rhino/Grasshopper, Revit/Dynamo, GSA™, Excel, with more applications such as Civil3d™ and Tekla applications in the pipeline.

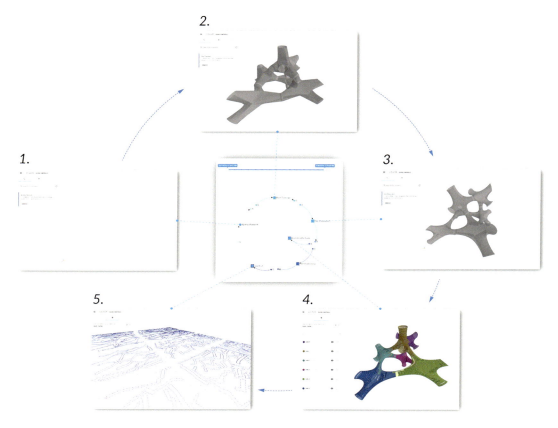

▲ Figure 3.33

Users can visualise data exchanges and access each "stream" (or data container) within the Speckle viewer environment, from the design to the fabrication stages.
© Poinet, P., Stefanescu, D., and Papadonikolaki, E.

3.7 Design Technology, Semiotics, and Human Behaviour!

OMA's Rem Koolhaas recently started to speculate on a post-Anthropocene future where the design of buildings less and less needs to consider humans and instead focus on the needs of machines that operate giga-factories, warehouses, and data centres.[36] In one example, Koolhaas responds to this utopia by

---

36 Koolhaas, R. (2019) 'Museum in the Countryside', in *Machine Landscapes: Architectures of the Post Anthropocene*, AD March 2019. Vol. 89. Issue 1, Wiley, Oxford, pp. 60–65.

juxtaposing the functional and machine-centric design of a data centre with that of a countryside museum, speculating about the *purity of intention, undistorted by architectural vision.*

In contrast to Koolhaas's musing over the post-Anthropocene future, most architects still firmly have their eye on designing for humans and thereby on exploring the human condition. Workspace design has become a major 'battleground' for large architecture firms. New modes of collaboration, paired with more flexible office/space rental regimes have shaken up the property market since the second decade of the new millennium. Start-up culture and the emergence of shared-workspace outlets is putting pressure on those designing and managing the related environments, which themselves have become highly optimised environments. The effects of COVID have further led to a rethink in Workspace planning, as employees seek more flexible models for working from home and/or the office (or other solutions).[37] In response to these market challenges, some architecture firms have started appointing dedicated workplace leaders who specialise in the design of such environments. Workspace has become 'big business' for architects and interior designers. One might ask what role does Design Technology play in this context?

In the past, attributes of human well-being and productivity have mainly been attested to qualitative and aesthetic characteristics of workspace design. This approach is slowly changing. Clients have become highly sensitised about the performance of their buildings, not just from an operational cost perspective but in terms of their impact on the productivity of their occupants. Automated sensors capture a plethora of different types of information about a building and feed back valuable insights to those operating it. Data analytics is then used to help optimise how a building and its occupants perform. This is where Design Technology comes in to establish a correlation between social/psychological behaviour and quantitative data via simulation and analysis in a spatial context.

The Bjarke Ingels Group, Foster + Partners have all set up Workspace teams to tackle these issues, with ZHA's Patrik Schumacher pushing the agenda furthest with a dedicated research group at the University of Applied Arts (Angewandte)[38] in Vienna on 'Agent-based Parametric Semiology'. There, they look at codified conventions of human interaction processes in a spatial context and use agent-based computational modelling to inform their space planning. The difference from previous and often single-purpose, agent-based modelling processes (such as egress models in fire/smoke spread simulations), Parametric semiology allows for more emergent behaviour to be included. Agents' paths do not simply depend on a predefined genetic algorithm, but they adapt and change behaviour based on more complex criteria that closely simulate individual human characteristics.

In parallel with Schumacher's studies on design semiology, Case Inc., and later WeWork,[39] conducted intensive studies on this subject to assist in maximising space utilisation, thereby deploying Machine Learning algorithms to test and predict occupancy levels.

---

37 WorkProud (2021) *Remote Work Is Here to Stay: How to Create a Win-Win Strategy for Your Organization and Employees.* Available at: https://workproud.com/remote-work-is-here-to-stay/ (Accessed: 31 October 2022).
38 Available at: http://i-o-a.at/research/ (Accessed: 31 October 2022).
39 Available at: www.wework.com/ideas/office-design-space/designing-with-machine-learning (Accessed: 31 October 2022).

▲ Figure 3.34

Digital Twin, gathering employee-related data affected by the office environment.
© Proving Ground

Most of these examples focus on Workspace design as a very specific market for architecture firms. Yet the bigger picture clearly points towards wider opportunities in the use of Design Technology for testing and simulating human behaviour in a spatial context. Many quantitative functional and environmental (performance) considerations could be analysed and optimised in the past via computational means. Now it seems we have reached a point where tools are increasingly able to help designers codify qualitative design aspects in order to provide useful performance feedback for their design in close to real time.

Chapter 4

Moving Forward

The concluding chapter of this book offers thoughts to scrutinise the current state of technology adoption by architecture firms, as well as some daring predictions on what the future of Design Technology might hold. In order to examine these issues through different lenses, four global industry leaders share their insights without holding back with critical reflection and pointed provocations. They have been – each in their own right – at the forefront of Design Technology innovation via publications, contributions to international guidelines and standards, and executed work.

Interview With Four Leading Design Technologists

Daniel Davis is a Brooklyn-based senior researcher at HASSELL where his primary focus lies in investigating 'workplace'. More generally, Daniel is a prolific author and provocateur who aims to unearth the ever changing context of technology, architecture, and people.

Nathan (Nate) Miller runs The Proving Ground from Omaha. The firm doubles up as a Design Technology consultancy and fertile ground for experimentations in digital, data-driven design. Nathan and his team are responsible for numerous plug-ins for Rhino/Grasshopper such as Lunchbox, Rhynamo, and Slingshot and support others in implementing Design Technology (strategies) into their practice.

Jon Mirtchin, founder of Geometry Gym, calls Victoria (Australia) his home and has been pivotal in advancing schemas that allow different software applications to communicate via common data definitions such as the international Foundation Classes (IFC, which Jon helps to advance).

Fabian Scheurer, co-owner of Zürich-based Design-to-Production is – in his own words – interested in neither one nor the other, yet he appears to be particularly keen to find ways to move across these two (sometimes separate) domains via smart interfaces and simple solutions, facilitated via technology.

As with many other commercial enterprises, Big Tech has also knocked on the door of the construction industry, hoping to disrupt the tool infrastructures currently in use via more flexible, data-centric platforms and user interfaces. Yet when it comes to our industry, surprisingly little seems to have changed. Has architecture survived the 'attack' of Big Tech?

Daniel: Some of the Tech companies like WeWork, Airbnb, and Sidewalk Labs [by Google] are definitely in trouble right now, but I would not be sighing in relief.

The architecture profession as a whole squandered the opportunity that technology offers. Rather than using technology to improve our businesses, to improve project outcomes, to create a better built environment, we have instead opted to find new ways to design curved walls. This creates major opportunities for all kinds of upstarts to come in and disrupt an ailing industry.

  Nate: Has architecture survived the attack of tech? I would say, yes! It happened by many practices, quite frankly, doing nothing. If we look at the last forty years leading up to this, the incentive for massive transformation, to completely overhaul processes has been low. At the Proving Ground we have seen a trend in uptake on owners engaging us for high level strategy, customisation, and standards development. What they are starting to experience, is that the products clients receive from architects, builders, and fabricators are not matching up with their new expectations. There is now downward pressure from those investing in buildings, as they have expectations that the performance of buildings should be more measurable and that the delivery process should be less wasteful and costly.

  Fabian: Nathan is absolutely right. It is not so much about whether architecture has survived Tech, it is more about: have they survived at all, and what role is technology playing in that? Architects and builders are somehow mingling through, and either they make too much profit to feel an urge for change or too little to invest in R&D at all. The building industry might look a bit different in Europe than it does in the US as we have many very small firms and only a few bigger ones, and real innovation is coming from neither end. Also, there is no real big tech industry here, so the 'Elon Musk of the building industry', who causes comparable turbulence like in the German car industry' probably needs to come from abroad.

  Jon: Only very few firms choose to disrupt themselves. It normally comes from an external force, be it intentional or unintentional. I think that is in agreement with all the previous comments. But otherwise, It is more of a slow evolution, which is where I see industry having travelled through my twenty years.

▼ Figure 4.1

Jon Mirtchin of Geometry Gym assisting students in applying IFC schemas for Rhino/Revit model data exchange.
© Dominik Holzer

This also leads to the next question: Why is it so hard to position Design Technology within firms?

Fabian: What we realised very distinctively at Design-to-Production is that a technology for the sake of technology does not really help anyone. The biggest problem we have in all the processes where we introduce new technology into existing workflows is that no one knows how to ask good questions for the models we produce. I found it very interesting to hear Nate talk about that because the whole thing is going to change if someone comes up with new questions to the process. Probably, then, we need new tools to come up with answers. If you have new tools and no new questions, that does not give you anything.

Nate: I'll address this question from a business model perspective. A lot of the difficulties that I have seen relate to how projects are executed and how businesses are organised around those projects. Profit margins in architecture firms tend to be slim. When firms start to introduce new processes, there is immediate scepticism in the sense that it starts to become disruptive to that cycle of project delivery. There are inherent or perceived risks about adopting new tools. If people are caught up in the tyranny of the urgent and the project delivery cycle, it is hard to think ten projects down the road in terms of what something's going to yield. If you do not understand what new question you are trying to ask, it becomes very hard to justify an investment in a new capability.

Daniel: WeWork head executives like Dave Fano who knew how the technology itself worked. They were able to ask the right questions and push forward. It did not hurt that we had a huge amount of capital, so we could make long-term investments in technology. We were basically doing the same project over and over again, so there was an incentive to improve the methods and improve the process since this yielded a better product at a lower cost. This is the opposite of what keeps occurring in many architecture firms, which is why they struggle in that regard.

How long before the asteroid crashes? When are we going to see tools that fundamentally change the way we operate, in particular when considering that most of the BIM tools currently on the market have been around for twenty (or so) years? In a way they are dinosaurs where additional features have been added over time, yet the way we work today might be totally different from back then.

Jon: Following on from the last discussion, there are a lot of chicken and egg effects in our industry. The reason we do not see a Revit killer is because contracts still basically demand drawings. Something needs to change: either contracts that prescribe the use of models as deliverables or an external drawing production tool. Both of those might happen. To produce technical drawings, to reproduce the kind of code Revit is based on, would be a lot of effort. That is not really the future.

Fabian: The elephant in the room is that we are talking technology and models and big data, whilst in the end, we are still expected to deliver a batch of 2D drawings on paper. Design-to-Production has been building models and providing digital fabrication for CNC-machines for the past fifteen years, but to do that we had and still have to misuse and extend the existing planning tools with hand-written code. And we typically are working on the side of the contractor because everything else would be contractually difficult, to say the least. I am still waiting for the point in time where we stop talking about file-based drawing delivery. For me, that will be the first step for a killer app – get rid of everything that is file based. It is a business model question and a question about responsibilities and legal issues.

Nate: The Revit killer, as everyone is saying here, is a fundamental change in procurement, contracting, and responsibility among the various parties within the building industry. What drives Revit adoption at the moment is your market inertia. It is very heavily marketed, very widely adopted. To get people to change from such a big investment is no short order. You are talking about people overhauling their standards, their entire working processes, and production cycles.

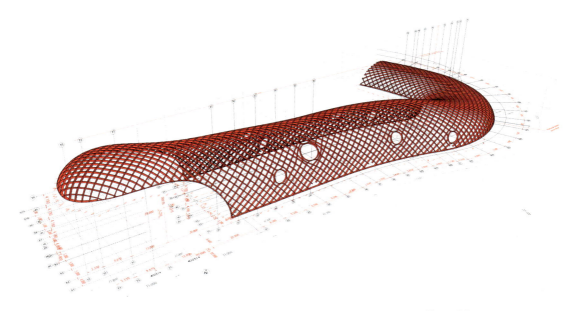

▲ Figure 4.2

Swatch building – roof shape optimised for fabrication.
© Design-to-Production

Are we currently underestimating or overestimating the value of BIM in terms of what it can offer to architects? On one hand, they are often not tying well into output from early design processes. On the other hand, we do not yet seem to fully capitalise on their ability to link data across our work processes.

Daniel: The way BIM is currently conceived of is a complete waste of time! You put a whole bunch of data into the model and hand it over to someone and just hope that they find something useful to do with the data. It is not driven by needs. It is a shame, as there is a lot of potential value in the data. For instance, if we were able to model data consistently across projects and keep it up to date with the building's life cycle, this would allow a client (or the designer) to learn about the performance of the building and learn about the performance of the design process. But instead, we just tick boxes to say we are doing BIM.

▼ Figure 4.3

Data extraction from BIM models (Workplace) for trend analysis across the portfolio.
© HASSELL

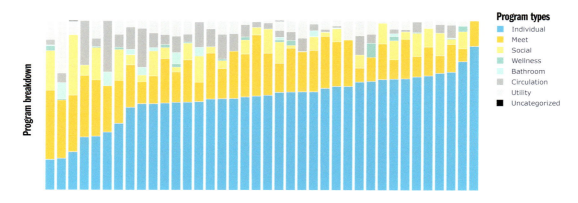

Fabian: The big question still is: what's the question? As long as we do not find a way of talking about the philosophy behind building digital models in a way that turns out qualitatively good data, BIM is doomed to producing gigabytes of information that end up in the bin. It is nice to have it on the way, maybe. It is answering some questions, but there is a dead end at some point. If you have a big CNC machine that wants to be precise, down to half a millimetre, then you need to have a model that is at least ten times as precise as that, to feed it with fabrication data.

Jon: At the moment, most of BIM is a push transaction. Someone creates data and pushes it to everyone else. If we get to pull a 'query transaction', BIM becomes a lot more powerful. What we really need are information models that we can query and pull the data we know we want from, rather than the current transactions.

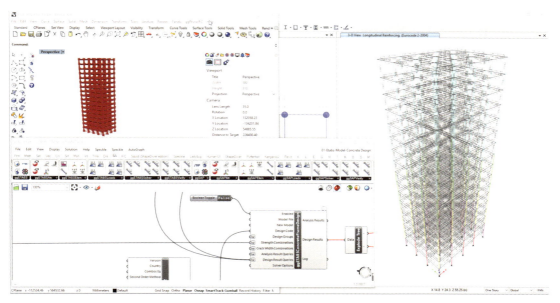

▲ Figure 4.4

Grasshopper to ETABS – schema for parametric optimisation of loadings in multistorey building design.
© Geometry Gym

Architects do not really think about this issue too deeply. We just try to get the work done, get the documentation out, because that is what we are getting paid for.

Fabian: As long as it is perfectly okay to end up with documentation that is inherently inconsistent and no one is going to notice until the 'very end guy' who tries to put two bricks on top of each other in two different directions, from two different documents. That is the problem.

It is easy to generate vast amounts of information, the expensive thing is to throw away information and keep the right one. That is what architects need to get better at.

In that context: is technology going to assist us with making more informed choices, in particular where vast amounts of information are involved? We increasingly see facets of our life being supported

(some might say 'controlled') by Artificial Intelligence (AI). It appears a number of architects and academics have investigated its potential for our industry. Yet there does not seem to be much evidence it is having a major impact on how/what we design. Are Machine Learning (ML) and AI (still) a thing?

Nate: ML and AI are 'still a thing' in the sense that they are very much on the lips of executives in architecture and construction practices. No one has quite figured out how, within the context of their firm, this might boost productivity. Accepting that Machine Learning is dependent on good training data to create effective learning algorithms that can help facilitate prediction, it has exposed for the firms that we are working with how much data they have and how poorly that data is manifested. Maybe we should have Machine Learning as a background janitor, instead of a front-end 'flashy thing' that you put in front of a client. That might be much harder to sell to an architect than a sexy algorithm.

Daniel: When you look at the buildings that are designed, it is outrageous how similar everything is and how much we do things over and over and over. There is so much repetitive work that intelligent tools could handle for designers. I am not talking about generative design tools that will produce a hundred different options that no one really understands. But by taking low-level parts of 'laying out a bathroom' or 'laying out a kitchen' and finding ways to automate that. The designer still remains in control, but there are these other agents in the drawing that are working away (like Nate's janitor analogy), making sure that things are going in the right direction.

There is another question associated to analysis: when it comes to these technologies, I am always curious what their endgame is and why we apply them. Are we only doing this to save time, or is there something more we can get from them? As an industry, we need to better understand how space affects the people that inhabit it. Why not apply this machine intelligence to these gaps in our knowledge? To me, that is the real issue to unlock.

Jon: For Machine Learning, you really need big data, which often is not accessible. You really do not even want data, you want information, which is structured data. If every project or every company has a different standard, that becomes part of the frustration in trying to interpret that data. Having more common standards and consistency would at least start to accelerate the use of automation in a way that makes it more powerful.

As designers, do we need to learn to automate in better ways than we currently do?

Nate: This goes back to a set of values and priorities when it comes to a design firm and its understanding of automation. The benefits of automation in the classic sense is that, for example, you have a set of processes, and you are able to encapsulate those set of processes into an algorithm or some type of faster process that reduces the amount of waste in the system. As a result, you start to see measurable increases in productivity, value added per worker. Architects have not quite looked at what productivity really means for their business practice; they have no baseline for measuring it. Therefore, when you start to introduce automation, It is like, 'Oh, we are going to bring in this thing that is going to take this very wasteful task, and make it less wasteful'. What do you mean less wasteful? Do we really understand how wasteful it is to begin with? Can we somehow create that measure of performance to understand what the impact of automation can be and therefore drive what we want to automate as a result?

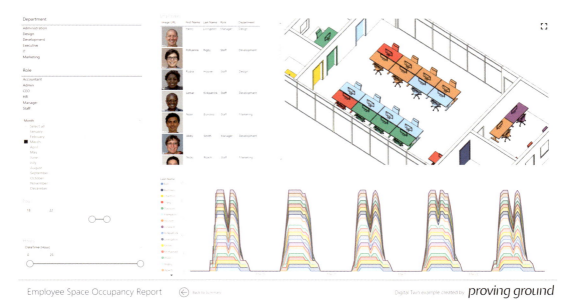

▲ Figure 4.5

Example of Digital Twin 'Employee space occupancy report'.
© Proving Ground

How can firms decide whether to do something in-house or have a third-party A team, who are specialised in giving particular input?

Fabian: Maybe that is a question of scale. Either you are big enough to keep a twelve-people specialist modelling group busy like Foster's does, or you are an architect that builds something crazy curvy every three years. That holds true for all specialisations. Either you have the guys in-house and you keep them busy and entertained, or they leave you and found a specialist company that you can then hire back at some point. It is a question of business model mainly.

Jon: I tend to agree with Fabian. If your expert is a one-man-team and that person leaves you, such a scenario leaves you very vulnerable as well. That scale question is very pertinent about where you draw the line with this. And Nate, you seem to be working, though, on a broader level on introducing a different scale of practices to different aspects of Design Technology.

Nate: This question of outside experts is one that always comes up as. 'Why do you need a consultant? Why do you need a specialist to tell you kind of a direction?' Part of the reason why you would do that relates to an understanding of a broader marketplace. Architecture firms in different contexts can be quite insular and protective of certain ideas or ways of working. They may be looking for some kind of outside perspective to understand what is happening in the marketplace. What trends are you seeing when you are working with an owner, which can impact our business model? That forms part of the value that we bring in. The value of a third-party objective opinion and knowledge set that can help influence where they might go next.

Daniel: On the research side, it is always about do you have the capability hiring someone who has got those skills, because firms may not have enough interesting projects or do not have the datasets to entertain this approach. Sometimes it makes sense to outsource research just because different firms specialise in it, and they can do it faster and better than you could do it in house. Sometimes it makes more sense to develop that IP internally. It is always about striking a balance.

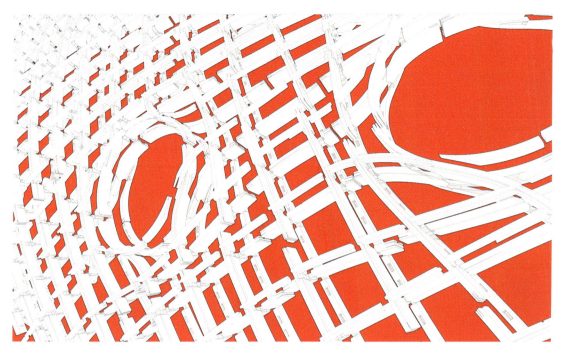

▲ Figure 4.6
Swatch building – 3D fabrication model.
© Design-to-Production

▲ Figure 4.7
Swatch building under construction.
© SJB Kempter Fitze AG

Fabian, in a recent publication you argued that educating the client is a key component to achieving better narrative of a project's digital story, particularly in the context of file-to-factory.

Fabian: Yes, we finally start to discuss how things need to change in order to avoid ending up with uncoordinated data for fabrication. Project teams need to ask themselves, 'How do we sort this process in a way that the right questions are posed at the right time?' This may not necessarily fit into the typical work stages proposed by the RIBA or other industry bodies because they are mainly built around on-site building and not off-site prefabrication. With Design-to-Production, we are used to coming in very late and working for the fabricators in almost 80% of our project, which typically involves taking all the digital data that comes (if there is any), throwing it away, and rebuilding it. Swatch would be one notable exception, where we were involved pre-tender as a consultant and modelling specialist. We managed to have a series of digital models that were started before tender and went all the way down to fabrication. Everybody's talking about that digital chain going from design straight down to CNC manufacturing. There are still so many missing links in there, on very different levels of the process.

Jon: What's being said is quite accurate; a significant influence on throwing away the data and starting again is because it is unstructured data. Informed clients that understand where the advantages to be gained on their projects would demand and validate upon receipt structured information. The effort required to reverse-engineer data and the risk in quality of resultant information typically lead to a project participant to start from scratch; this is particularly relevant to fabricators.

What will be the main impact of Design Technology in the next ten to twenty years?

Daniel: Jon said earlier that the industry is not going to disrupt itself, and I agree. In the next ten years, if there's going to be a big change, I do not expect that it will come from inside the industry. I look at what's happening with Google, Katera, or Airbnb. These are the early warning shots, the signal the tech industry has architecture in its crosshairs. Some design firms are going to work out a new model and manage to compete. But others are going to struggle, and I can imagine tech companies taking entire sectors away from traditional practices.

▼ Figure 4.8

Survey of 2,300 people to identify post-COVID workplace preferences.
© HASSELL

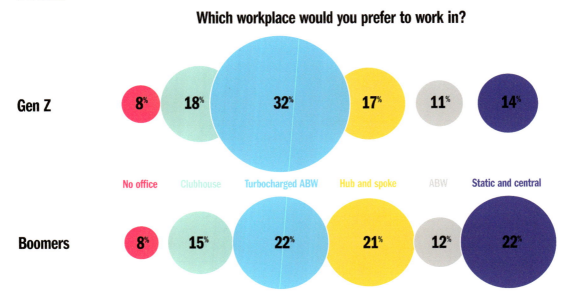

CHAPTER 4 Moving Forward

Nate: What we are seeing and feeling is that the transformations that allow for meaningful change and the transformation to take hold are going to be driven by increased savviness on behalf of stakeholders who are investing in buildings, and those operating/maintaining them. Larger players (developers and such) are now increasing their expectations of data-based deliverables and integrations with other systems. That expectation is now being driven down that supply chain, which might lead to business model changes. Another possible future is that absolutely nothing's going to happen in the next ten to twenty years; maybe the difference is very little ten years from now if we follow that trend line. Let's hope something might happen.

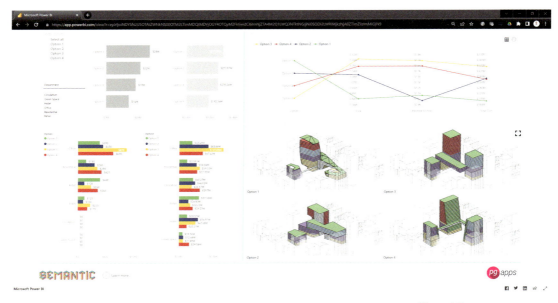

▲ Figure 4.9

Visualising revenue and cost options during the master planning stage via Power BI using 'Semantic'.

© Proving Ground

Fabian: I agree with both of you! There needs to be outside pressure to change things in the architectural industry. If this is now coming from above [the client] or from other factors, I do not think that the architects will disrupt their own industry. The big problem of the building industry is that it does not scale well in terms of digital processes as soon as you have to move items (not only bits). But it is also very hard to scale things. It is an inherently local industry; buildings are very rarely shipped around, and it is inherently over-regulated, at least in the place I am close to.

Jon: I have no crystal ball, but what I really hope is that the design tech we get in the next ten to fifteen years is automating all the labourious, repetitive stuff that no one enjoys doing and allows us as humans to use that creative thinking and those design skills to develop better built environments. It is going to be exciting.

Index

Note: Page numbers in *italics* indicate a figure.

2D 10, 15–16, 29–30, 85, 99; CAD
    29, 59; documentation 4, 128,
    131; drawings 98, 147
3D files 131, 138; model /
    modelling xiii, 6, *12*, 13, 17, 29,
    31, 55, 58, 80, 86, 88, 122, 124,
    128–129, 132; print / printer /
    printed ix, *52*, 74, *82*, 83, 85, *85*,
    87; scan / scanner / scanned 90,
    123; software 60, 130

ABACUS 30
academia / academic ix–xii, 28–29,
    39, 49, 51, 68, 134, 137, 139, 150
agent 138, 150; based 50, 143
algorithm 8, 28, 68, 79, 103–104,
    117, 124, 143, 150
analysis 2, 9, 22, *24*, 25, 32, *32*,
    54–55, 68, 73, 78, 99, *100*, 104,
    109, 111, 114, 132, 143, *148*,
    150; data 103; environmental 30,
    31, 116, 134; structural 30, *31*,
    136
Application Programming Interface
    (API) 102, 115
application xi, xiii–xiv, 3, 14–17, 20,
    26, 28–32, 41, 44–45, 50, 57,
    64, 68–69, 78, 80, 86, 91–92,
    101–104, 115–117, 122–124,
    122, 126, 131, 141–142, 145
ArchiCAD 29
architect / architects ix–x, xiii, xv,
    1–3, 6, 16–17, 20, 24, 28, 30–32,
    37, 40–43, 45, *48*, 49, 51, 54–55,
    59, 67, 78–81, 86, *89*, 90, 92–93,
    101, 103, 122–123, 127–129,
    131–132, 134, 143, 149–151, 154
Architectural Association (AA)
    72, 134
ARD 20, 22, 24, *25–26*, 26–27

Artificial Intelligence (AI) xii, 13, 93,
    100, 104, 150; *see also* Machine
    Learning (ML)
Arup xi, 14, 68–69, *110*
Augmented Reality (AR) xiii, 2,
    21, 27, *35*, 37, 109, 118–119,
    121–122, *121*, *124*, *126*, 137
AutoCAD 16, 64, 76, 99
Autodesk (ADSK) 16, 29, 80, 102,
    104, 114, 115
automation / automate 3, 10, 14,
    30, *31*, 40, 68, 81, 103–105,
    111–112, 116–117, 119, 124,
    128–130, 132, 134–135, 138,
    141, 143, 150, 154

Baroque 41
Bartlett (School of Architecture) 72
Bentley 16, 28–29, 87, 102
BIMbeats 91, *91*
Bjarke Ingels Group (BIG) xii, 32,
    34–40, 35–37, 39–40, 67, 69,
    112, 143
Building Information Modelling
    (BIM) xiv, 2, 7, 11, 13, 16, *19*, 21,
    25, 30, 36–40, *36*, *38*, 44–45, 51,
    64, 67–70, 73–77, 83, 90–92, *91*,
    100–102, 109, 111, 119, 121,
    124–126, *125*, 128–129,
    147–149; execution plan xi,
    80–81; manager 60, 73, 81, 92,
    124; model 86, 98, *148*
business xi, xiv, 44, 45, 50, 55, 57,
    66, 69, 92–93, 92, 102, 115–116,
    127, 132, 143, 146–147,
    150–151, 154

C++ 68
CATIA 28, 49, 60, 62–64, *86*, 87,
    128, 132, 138

China 12, 88, 96, 98, 130, 138

client 4, 7, 30, 36, 42, 44, 62, 64, 68, 78–81, 93, 101, 108, 135, 143, 146, 148, 150, 153–154

CNC 51–52, 74, 122, *123*, 124, *125*, 131, 134, 147, 149, 153

Code 55, 129, 131–132, 147

CODE – ZHA Computation and Design Group 47–51

collaboration xi, 24–25, 27, 36, 39, 42, 54, 72, *73*, 74, 77, *77*, 79, 86, 99, 107, *109–110*, *112*, 117–118, 126, 128, 132, 143

complexity / complex xi, 3, 8, 12, 14, *19*, *23*, 26, 28, 43, 47, 53, 65, 68, 83, 87, 98, 104–105, 117, 126, 128–129, 131–132, 134–135, 140, 143; geometric 11, 22

computational 7–8, 10, 15, 18, 28, 30–31, 36–37, 79, 93, 105, 116, 143–144; design 2, 14, 22, 24, 35, 39, 59, 68–69, 72–74, 102–103, 141

computational fluid dynamics (CFD) 31, *32*, 116

computer x–xi, 1–4, 14–18, 22, 51, 57, 60–61, 68, 80, 84–85, 87, 96, 99, 102–103, 105, 127–131, 141

computer aided design (CAD) x, 15–17, 29–30, 45, 57–58, 64, 76, 91, 99, 102, 122, 128, 131

construction xi, 7–8, 13–16, 18, 24, 30, 42–43, 74, 76, 78, 80–81, 85, 88, 92, 100, *113*, 119, *122–123*, 126, 129–131, *133*, 134–135, 138, 140–141, 145, *152*

Construction Operation Building Information Exchange (COBie) 81

consultancy / consultant xi, 4, 6, 11, 21–22, 36–37, 44, 51, 56, 67, 86–87, 92, 95, 134, 145, 151, 153

contractor 4, 6, 11, 20, 30, 42, 44, 51–52, 56, 68, 78–79, 88, 92–93, 128–130, 134, 147

convergence xiv, 54, 79, 141, 141

Coop Himmelb(l)au 4–13, *5–9*, *11–12*, 43, 67, *130*

Corbusier (Le) 42

cost xi, 27, 30, 37, 44–45, 48, 51, 53–54, 57, 67–68, 78, 90, 118, 129, 132, 134, 140, 143, 146–147, 154

COVID xiii, 36, 39, 117, 119, 143, *153*

craft ix, 42–43, 59, 72–73, *73*, 75, 77, 87, 102, 110

creative / creativity xv, 2, 20, 24, 41–42, 57, 62, 75, 87–88, 93, 99, 111, 154

culture / cultural xiii–xiv, 3, 7, 11, 22, 25, 33, 41, 55, 55, 60, 65, 74–75, 85, 88, 93, 96–97, 102, 105, 108, 117, 123, 134, 138, 143

data xi, xiii, 2, 16–17, 30, 49, 54–55, 68, 73, 76, 81, 90–92, 103–105, 111, 114, 116, 128–129, 142–143, *142*, *144*, 145, *146*, 147–151, *148*, 153–154; design 15, 141, 149

deconstructivism / deconstructivist 43

Design–to–Production *131*, 145, 147, *148*, *152*, 153

digital xi–xiv, 1–3, 6–8, 10, 13–14, 16, 18, 28, 42–44, 47, 52–54, 56–57, 60–61, 70, 72–77, *73*, 83–84, 87, *95*, *100*, 102–103, 105, 110, *118*, 120–121, *123*, 124–125, 127–128, *138*, 141, 145, 153, 154; fabrication 7, *50*, *76*, 134, 147; model 5, 11, 21, 30, 30, 58, *76*, 107–*108*, 122, *138*, 149, 153; twin *144*, *151*; workflow 3, 56, 125

Diller Scofidio + Renfo (DS+R) x, xii, 57–65, *57*, *61*, *63*, 67, 132

disruptive 49, 51, 121, 147

Diva 32

documentation xi, xiii–xiv, 2–3, 6, 15–16, 29–30, 29, 39, 44, 54, 64, 67, 70, 75–76, 79–81, 87, 99, 103, 117–118, 125–126, 128–129, 131, 138, 149

drawing / drawing ix, xi, 2, 4, 16, 29, 51, 59, 60–61, 64, 76, 81, 83–84, 86, 88, 98, 103, 111, 121, 135, 138, 140, 147, 150

Dynamo 39, 68, 91, 104, 111–112, 142

engineer / engineering ix, xi, 4, 22, 28, 30–31, 37, 41–43, 48, 51, 54–56, 63–64, 69, 78–79, 81, 86, 92, 96, 99, 103–104, *107–108*, 129, 132, 141, 153; digital xiv, 16; structural 8, 75

environmental 30–32, 30, 35, 54, 68, 73, 76, 78, 116, 132, 134–135, 140, 144

Europe 39, 95, 134, 146

experiment / experimental 1, 4, 6, 14–15, 17–18, 20, 29–30, 36–37, 43, 56, 63, 66, 69, 72, 85, 96, 101, *121*, *124*, 137, 140, 145

fabrication xiii–xiv, 2–3, 6–9, 13–14, 18, 43–44, *50*, *52*, 54, 67–70, 73–76, *76*, 78–79, 86, *98*, 103, 107–108, 128, 128, 129–132, *129*, *131*, 134–135, 139–140, *142*, 147, *148*, 149, *152*, 153

fabricator 6, 43, 51–53, 67, 72–74, 76, 78, 84, 95, 98, 128–132, 146, 153

Food4Rhino 68, 116

formwork *134–137*, 138, 140

Foster + Partners xii, *16*, 18, *19–20*, 20–28, *23–26*, 67–69, 143

G–Code 131

Geco 31

Ge–CoDe 70, 73–77

generative 28, 103–105, 115–116, 150

genetic 143

geometric / geometrical 8, 11, 17–18, 20, 28–30, 43, 49, 51, 54, 63–64, 68, 95, 97, 111, 128–131

geometry xi, 17–18, 22, 28–30, *29*, *31*, 32, 44, 51, *52*, 53, 60, 68, 72–76, *75*, 78–79, 87, 96, 99, 103, 111, 114–115, 126, 128–129, 131–133, 141, 145, *146*, *149*; Gym *31*, 111, 145, *146*, *149*

Graphisoft 29

Grasshopper 7, 28, 31–32, 37, 39–40, 49, 63, 68, 73, 76, 79, 87, 90, 95, 97–99, 102–104, 111–112, 115–116, 131–132, 138, 142, 145, 149

group 7, 10, 14–15, 20–22, 24, 26, 28–30, 32, 34, 35–37, 44, 50–51, 53–54, 60, 66–70, 74, 79, 92, 102, 108–109, 111–112, 122–124, *123*, 141, 143, 151

hardware 3, 7, 16, 26, 45, 56, 65, 80, 90, 97, 118

HASSELL 67, 69, 145, *148*, *153*

Heatherwick Studio xii, *32*, 67, 69–77, 71, *73–77*

Herzog & de Meuron / H&deM xii, 67, 119–127, *120–126*

High–Tech 20, 43

Hololens 25, 77, 122

Hypar 116

industry xiii–xiv, 24–25, 27, 40, 42, 47, 49, 51, 53, 88, 92, 114, 118–119, 130–131, 135, 145–147, 150, 153–154

Information Technology (IT) xi, 3, 37, 60, 67, 90, 109, 111, 117

innovation xi, 3–4, 9, 14, 20, 22, 24, 26, 35, 41–43, 53, 56, 62, 66, 75, 87, 96, 107–109, 111, 127, 145–146

innovative 6, 8, 20, 59, 68, 77, 92–93, 134

input xiii, 3, 11, 17, 22, 24, 28, 41, 45, 59, 66–69, 79–81, 99–100, *110*, 121, 123, 141, 151

Institute for Advanced Architecture of Catalonia (IAAC) *29*, 72, *73*

Kabinett 121, 126, *126*

Karamba 30

Ladybug 32, 116

LASSA xii, 67, 132–140, *133–139*, 133

leadership xiv, 44–45, 57, 66–67, 69–70, 79, 90–91, 90, 105, 107, 111, 116, 124

limitation 12, 16–18, 25, 39, 51, 53, 65, 77, 88, 99–100, 127, 140

Machine Learning (ML) ix, 73, 104, 105, *105*, 143, 150; *see also* Artificial Intelligence (AI)

INDEX

manage xiv, 1, 7, 49, 53, 64, 78, 81, 84, 107, 116, 153

manual / manually 60, 79, 98, 104, 125

MASH 116

McNeel 17, 28, 30, 68, 102, 115

Melbourne xi, xii, *109–110, 113, 129*, 132

Microsoft 104, 117, 137

Miro 107, 117, *118*

Mixed Reality 13, *38*, 74, 77, 80

model xiii, 3, *5–6, 6–7, 8,* 9–10, *12, 15,* 21, 24, 36–37, 47, 55–57, 60–61, *63,* 68, 70, 75, *76,* 79, 81, 86, 99, 102, *109,* 111, 116, 118–119, 122, 126–127, *126,* 129, 140, *146,* 147–149, 151, 153–154

modelling ix, 2, 6, 9, 16, 20–22, 25, 28–30, *31,* 32, 44, 50, 53–54, 59, 68–69, 75–78, 80–81, 90–91, 95, 99, 104, *110,* 115, 117, 122, 124, 143, 151, 153; software 17, 100, 129

modernism / modernist 26, 42–43

Morphosis Architects x, xii, 43, 67, 81–89, *82–89,* 82

object–oriented 2, 29–30, 29, 54, 80, 129

Octopus 104

office ix–x, xiv, 3, 6–7, 9, *10,* 12, 20, 22, 24–26, 33, 35–37, 39, *40,* 51, 56, 59, 61, 63–67, *66,* 69, 79–81, *83–84,* 84–85, 88, 90, 95, 97, 99–100, 117–118, *117,* 122, 126, 134, 137–139, 143, *144*

optimisation xiv, 7–8, 15, 22, 28, 54, 69, 72, 78, 86–87, 103–104, 116, *149*

optimise 9, 11, 30, 49, 75, 105, 143–144, *148*

organisation 6, 11, 44, 91, 107–108

organisational xi, xiv, 3, 6, 21, 36, 55–56, *66,* 66, 69, 73, 78, 84–85, 92, 108, 122, 136

OXSYS 15

parameter 79, 81, 88, 99, 103–104, 115, 141

parametricism 44, 47, 53

parametric ix, xiv, 2, *19,* 22, *23,* 28, 30–32, 44, 50, 55, 63, 68, 78, 87, 114, 143, *149*; model 6, 28, *31,* 69, 75, 79

performance xiv, 7–9, *10,* 14–15, 20, 22, 28, 30, 32, 35, 47, 54–55, 57, 68–69, 78, 90–91, 99, 103–104, *110,* 115–116, 135, 141, 143–144, 146, 148, 150

performative 102

philosophy 41, 43, 45, 51, 55, 57, 149

Photoshop 17, 59, 61–63, *61,* 65, 99

physical *5,* 6, 9–11, *10,* 24, 30, 55, 72–74, 77, *94–95,* 117, 124, *124,* 126, *126,* 130; model 3, 6, *8,* 10, *12,* 21, 29, 36, 60, 70, 95, 97, 99–100, 118–119, 121, 126, 137, 140

plug–in 16, 28, 35, 39, 44, 54–55, 68, 76, 102–103, 115–116, 128, 145

post–modern 43

practice ix–xiv, 2–4, 6, 12, 14–18, *14,* 20–22, 24–25, 27–32, 35, 40–45, *41,* 47–48, 51, 53, 55–57, 66–69, 72–73, 75–76, 79, 83–85, 90–93, *90,* 95–97, 99–105, 107, 115–118, 121, 124, 128, 132, 134–135, 137, 141, 145–146, 150–151, 153

productivity xi, 16, 30, 45, 56, 92, 103, 117, 130, 143, 150

project xi, xiii, xiv, 2–3, 6–18, 20, 22, 27–30, 35–37, 39, 42–45, 47–50, *50,* 53–58, 60–69, 72–80, *78,* 83, 85–88, *85, 88,* 90–97, *94–95,* 95–105, 107–109, 111–113, 115, 118, 121–124, 126–129, 131–132, 134–135, *135,* 137–141, *140,* 146–148, 150–151; teams 24, 32, 51, 61, 75, 79, 81, 92, 97, 105, 111, 123, 153

proliferation xiv, 3, 28, *28,* 30, 55, 93, 102, 115, 119

prototype / prototypes 7, *29,* 70, 73, 75, 86–87, *107–108,* 112, *125,* 134, 139

Proving Ground (the) *105, 144,* 145–146, *151, 154*

R&D 22, 27, 37, 48, 90, 109, 139, 146
render / rendering / rendering ix,
   17, 45, *47*, 55, *61*, 63, 65, *88*, 97,
   122, *123*, *125*, 126, 136
research xi, xiii, 7, 9, 14, 16, 20–22,
   24, 27–28, 49–51, 66–68, 72–75,
   77, 83, 96, 104, 108–109, 124,
   130, 134, 139–140, 143, 145, 151
Revit 11, 25, 29, 36, 39, 51, 60,
   62–64, 76, 87, 99–100, 104, 109,
   109, 111–114, 127, 138, 142,
   146, 147
Rhino 7, 10, 17, 25, 28, 30, 32,
   51, 62, 64, 73, 76, 79, 87, 95,
   97–100, 102, 109, 111, 114–116,
   125–128, 131–132, 138, 140,
   142, 145, *146*
Rhino Inside 39, 68
RIBA *15*, 153
risk ix, 52–53, 56, 85, 88, 90, 101,
   119, 121, 130, 139, 147, 153
robot / robotics 2, 6–7, *26*, 30,
   52, 74, 100, *125*, 128–129, *130*,
   131–132, 139–141
RUCAPS 16
Ruskin 42–43, 57

scripting ix, xi, xiv, 2, 7, 16, 18, 25,
   28, 28, 54, 68, 101–104, *110*,
   116, 122, 124, 135
semiotics / semiology 50, 142, 143
SimScale 116
Sketch Design (SD) 39, 76
sketching 3, 7, 10, 26, 37, 41, 57,
   61, 70, 75–77, 80, 99–100, *118*,
   121, 125–127
SmartGeometry 28–29, *29*
software x–xi, 1, 3, 14–17, 26, 28–29,
   31, 43, 45, 51, 54–55, 57–58,
   62–65, 76, 80–81, 87, 90–91,
   100–102, 104, 109–110, 112, 114,
   116–118, 122, 124, 128–132, 134,
   139, 142, 145; design software 44,
   92, 102, 115, 141
SO–IL xii, 67, 93, 94–100, 94,
   94–100
solar 9, 31–32, *32*, 68
Solidworks 9, 31–32, *32*, 68
Spakermaker 104

Speckle 39, 113, 141–142, *142*
strategy / strategic xi, xiii–xv, 24–25,
   27, 44–45, 44, 54, 56, 66, 70, 84,
   90, 93, 95, 107, 109, 116, 143,
   145–146
structural 8, 11, 14, *15*, 30, 30, 31,
   31, 43, 48–49, 54, 64, *64*, 68, 75,
   78–79, 112, 128, 130–131, *131*,
   134, 136
structure xiii–xiv, 2–3, 7, 14, 22, 28,
   30, 33, 37, 41, 45, 50, 53–56, 60,
   63, 66–70, 74, 85, 90, 93, 97,
   101, 107, 109, 117, 121, 124,
   135, 137, 141, 145, 150, 153
studio / studios xi–xiv, 1, 3, 21–22,
   32, 33, 35, 39, 54–55, 59, 60–61,
   63–64, 67, 69–70, 71, 72–77,
   72–75, 104, 107–109, 111–113,
   126, 132, 134, 87, 95–96
superpositioning 56
support xiii–xiv, 1–3, 6, 12, 20–22,
   24–26, 28–30, 33, 35, 37, 39, 41,
   44, 49, 54–58, 55, 66–70, 75–81,
   78, 88, 90, 93, 95, 100–105, 103,
   109, 111, 114–117, 121, 123–125,
   127–128, 141, 145

team / teams xi, xiii, 3, 6,–7, 9,
   12–14, 16, 22, 24–26, *25–26*, 32,
   36–37, 39, 44, 47–51, 54, 57, 61,
   64, 66–70, 73–81, 85–86, 90–92,
   96–97, 105, 107–109, 111–112,
   117–119, 118, 120, 121–124,
   126–127, 129, 135, 141, 143,
   145, 151
techniques 2, 28, 43–44, 52, 68, 72,
   75, 85, 93, 95–96, 100, 131
Tekla 102, 142
TestFit 104, 116
tool / tools ix, xi, xiv, 1–3, 6–10,
   12–14, 16–17, 20, 22, 24–32,
   35–37, 39–41, 44–45, 48–49, 51,
   53–58, 60–62, 64–65, 68–69,
   72–74, 77–80, 84–88, 90–93,
   95–105, 101, 103, 107, 109, *110*,
   111–118, 121–122, 126–127, 129,
   131–132, 138–141, 141, 144–145,
   147, 150; ecology xiv, 47, 54–55,
   76, 79, 87, 125; selection xiv, 56

tooling 101, 141
training 16, 57, 69, 77, 81, 90, 91–92, *91*, 101, 109, 116–117, 150
transformation 83, 93, 124, 146, 154
transformative xiii, 2, 92

United States of America / USA 15, 146
university x–xii, 7, 14, *15*, 27, 30, 126, 143

Virtual Reality (VR) xiii, 6, 21, 27, 35–37, *35*, 51, 56–57, 80, *84*, 100, 109, 118–119, *120*, 121–122, 140

visualisation (Viz) xiii–xiv, 2–3, 17, 21, 27, 32, 35–37, 39–40, 69, 73, 75, 79–80, 90, 102–103, 111, 114, 118, 122
visualize 62, 75, 77, 91, 110, 126, *142*
visuals 17, 74, 79–80

workflow xi, 2, 17, 25, 28, 30, 36–37, 40, 45, 49–50, 54, 57, 68, 75–81, 85–87, 90, 92–93, 104, *105*, *110*, 111, *112*, 114–119, 124, 131–132, 137, 139, 141, 147
workplace 143, 145, *148*, *153*

Zaha Hadid Architects (ZHA) x, xii, 43, *44–53*, 45–53, 46